ANOTHER WAY O

By the same author

Lydia's Story

FRONT COVER: *Mariga, the Hon. Mrs Desmond Guinness*
BACK COVER: *The Mourne Mountains near Dundrum*

Lydia de Burgh

Another Way of Life

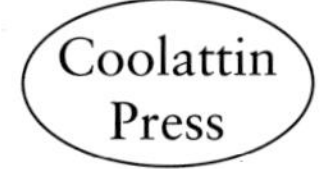

First published in 1999
by Coolattin Press
4 Church Court, Clough,
Downpatrick, Co. Down BT30 8QX
The publication of this book was assisted by the
Ulster Local History Trust

Printed in Northern Ireland by
Nicholson & Bass Ltd.

British Library Cataloguing in Publication Data

A catalogue record for this book is available from
the British Library

ISBN 0 9535937 0 3

CONTENTS

ILLUSTRATIONS

Front cover – Mariga, the Hon. Mrs Desmond Guinness, painting by Lydia be Burgh.

---

[1] By kind permission of Mrs Elise Coburn

[2] By kind permission of The Earl of Roden, her son.

[3] By kind permission of Mrs Jo Ottaway, née de Burgh

INTRODUCTION

SO MANY PEOPLE have written charming and amusing letters asking me to write another book, that somewhat doubtfully, I have now done so.

This one is not a chronological narrative but more a commonplace book about further lovely countries, customs, and people I have known, plus a few of the nasty ones! though not enough of the latter to make it a best seller I fear.

For those who have not read my autobiography 'Lydia's Story' I have included a few more family details, otherwise it is written in much the same way.

When in the 18th Century Madame de Sévigny wrote the letters to her daughter which became so famous, they were conversational ... a sharing of thoughts, jokes, troubles and gossip between the writer and reader. They were also informed and amusing. When I started to write this seemed the most natural way of doing so though I had not then read Madame de Sévigny. It seems to have succeeded in 'Lydia's Story' beyond my wildest dreams.

This time I hope the spelling and punctuation are more polished, and I have had the fascinating experience of learning the completely new to me business of publishing with all its rewards, frustrations, and very hard work. It greatly increases my admiration for other writers as the financial rewards for non-fiction are not great, and reading is one of my greatest pleasures.

I am greatly interested in people. This is perhaps why I am a successful portrait painter, and may be accused by a prejudiced few of name dropping. But unless one is completely obsessed with oneself it is really pointless to write a biography, much less an autobiography, without mentioning people by name. All those I mention were special to me in some way, or of interest to others. After all as Alexander Pope said more than two hundred years ago 'the proper study of mankind is man,' and I have certainly enjoyed the study!

Inevitably many biographies have to be written by people who did not know their subjects personally because they have been long dead. Very good they are, but the jokes, troubles, charm ... or lack of it ... and the 'aura' which brings a person to life is often missing. Writing about people who are still alive is far more difficult because one does not want to breach privilege or confidence, especially that of the Royal Family who are accorded almost no privacy at all and are often wildly and ludicrously misrepresented. Having had the honour of painting the Queen and others personally all the extremely interesting conversations, jokes and amusing anecdotes we shared ... they were never unkind ... have been written down separately and will be stored at the Records Office and elsewhere with a twenty year embargo on them.

I have dedicated this book to my beloved dogs and horse 'which I have loved long since and lost a while'.

ACKNOWLEDGEMENTS

NOW IT ONLY REMAINS for me to acknowledge my thanks everyone who assisted me in the task of writing this book.

Thanks to John Knipe for so kindly teaching me in his spare time how to use my mystifying word-processor and eliminating some of its nastier tricks. John also used his expertise in Desktop Publishing to produce the final 'copy' for the printers.

Thanks also to Patrick Cross my friend (and legal adviser) for reading the M.S. and encouraging me to go ahead with publishing; and Brian Kennedy Keeper of the Pictures at the Belfast Museum and author, for similar impartial encouragement. Also Bill de Burgh, cousin of Baramba, W. Australia for giving me copies of my de Burgh Grandparents' letters to his Grandfather.

To the memory of
'Sigi', 'Solo' and 'Button' my beloved Border Terriers
and 'Loveday' my little Bay mare.

*'Those angel faces ... which I have loved
long since and lost awhile.'*

John H. Newman

CHAPTER 1

THAILAND
1974 AND LATER

I learnt about Thai massage from a 'merchant of death'. Having always been addicted to massage for damage done when riding as a child, and later skiing, I was wary and dubious of embarking on it there. This was fortunate, for one day I was sharing the hotel minibus to the market in Hua Hin with a lively young man who came to Thailand quite often. He was a dealer in arms for a well-known firm. The subject of massage came up, so I begged for information.

'Well,' he said, 'There are two kinds of massage, you see ... hand massage and body massage.'

'Oh', I said, 'I don't just want my hands massaged.'

'Ah but wait a bit,' he replied laughing, 'Hand massage means they massage you all over by hand. Body massage means they massage the whole of your body with the whole of their body!' Help! ... I did a U turn, and firmly opted for hand massage.

The beauty attendants at the hotel health salon did not speak much English but I made an appointment, and, they told me helpfully 'Man massage man, and lady massage lady.'

It was not so. I stripped off in a pretty padded cell ... and in came a good-looking young man, all smiles. 'Oh', I said doubtfully 'Are you the masseur?' 'Yes' he replied 'I masseur, I also tennis coach!' I gave up. In fact he was extremely good ... at hand massage ... and I gathered Reception had got it wrong, and man massaged ladies and ladies massaged men. Or so they said.

Hand massage is not looked on as a luxury in the East and one quickly gets hooked on it. Even the hairdresser kneads the tension out of one's neck and shoulders as part of the treatment, and most households have a visiting masseuse once a week at least who does the whole family, or they do each other. Bliss. Imagine that happening here. In India however the sexes are discretely segregated. Massage parlours of course are something else again, and definitely not for ladies.

On my first visit to Thailand in 1973 Sylvia Forde, a friend and neighbour came too, but despite having between us a great selection of introductions to people there we got off to a bad start.

Being far from affluent, we had booked into an old but not at all smart hotel near the Royal Palace and temples.

The first night, still jet lagged from the then eighteen hours flight, we wandered out in search of dinner ... with no success. Normally there is flourishing wok cooking going on at every street corner, but we had turned the wrong way and found only a seedy looking place where mosquitos gnawed away at our ankles. Too tired to walk any further we ordered a Thai soup of great renown. This proved an utter disaster. In the first mouthful I found an enormous gold filling which fell out into the bowl with a loud clang. Mercifully it turned out to be my own. That was bad enough, but then horror of horrors, near the bottom of the bowl I found a small jawbone with a full set of teeth. Panic ensued. Was I disintegrating completely? Whose could they be? After careful exploration all mine still seemed to be intact. Then the awful truth dawned ... they were dog's teeth! – just like my beloved Border terrier's. By then we had almost finished the soup which actually tasted quite good. Totally demoralised and almost in tears, we tottered back to the hotel and gulped huge draughts of our duty free gin! Later we were told that in very poor areas everything went into the soup.

Next morning we set out on foot for the Royal Palace. The heat was tremendous, but once inside the high walls a world of magic lay before our eyes. The carved temples and pavilions had high twirling roofs which glittered with gold and jewel coloured tiles. Strange statues glittered too, and fierce stone dragons guarded the great doors. From whitewashed cloisters long lines of gilded Buddhas sat in timeless contemplation of their sunlight courtyards, shaded by slender trees. It was immaculately kept and at that hour almost deserted. We were enchanted, the horrors of the soup forgotten.

That night we put on our prettiest long frocks and dined at the Oriental. This famous hotel where Somerset Maugham and Alec Waugh once lived and wrote was then still quite small, and perfectly beautiful. The classic pillared front led into a lovely garden by the river, where we ate delicious food on the terrace and watched the rice barges with their painted eyes, and many other craft plying their trades. The air was balmy on our bare shoulders, and lights twinkled amongst the trees.

Greatly restored, we now took up some of our introductions. One of Sylvia's was to Kurt Wachtveitel, Manager of the Oriental, an attractive Swiss-German with a charming Thai wife. He promptly asked us to lunch next day. When he heard of our encounter with the dog soup he was much amused and asked 'But why are you not staying here?' ... and in no time at all we were, as guests of the management.

This was truly from the ridiculous to the sublime. Everything at the Oriental is arranged for beauty and delight, and there is no doubt that beautiful surroundings, wearing beautiful clothes and being treated as a beautiful person soon makes you feel like one. This is a great tradition in Thailand and part of its many charms.

We were now swept into a whirl of events. I met Pornsri Luphaiboon the public relations manager who quickly became a friend and was greatly interested in my Royal and other paintings. She arranged interviews with the Press and photographers and V.I.P. treatment in general. One's natural instinct is not to talk about one's achievements, but I soon learnt that a little publicity pays handsome dividends; also that no-one can 'promote' a person they know nothing about.

Pornsri also helped us greatly over sightseeing. We found we could do a lot of this by the river ferries which were much cooler and flew along in a cloud of spray. They cost only a few pence. It was necessary to get one's destination written down in Thai, and also of course the port of return. I then waved these at the driver, paid the incredibly small fare, and someone pushed us off at the correct stop. It was essential to write it down in English as well so that one knew which message one was brandishing. I ended up with a great collection which took me all over Bangkok for years, though not everyone could read or write.

The previous summer the Oriental had been the setting for much of the film 'The Man With the Golden Gun', a James Bond extravaganza which had given them several headaches. Kurt was very amusing about this. I asked him whether cars really could take off and jump canals ... klongs, as they did in the film. 'Oh yes, they do it frequently,' he replied laughing, 'The only difference is that they do not get to the other side!'

These waterways were one of the magical things about Thailand. Once the main thoroughfare for all market traffic for miles around, they formed a great network, originally running through most of Bangkok. The little flat boats paddled by women in wide brimmed hats and bright sarongs became favourite subjects for my paintings, and on the quiet country backwaters the scenery was beautiful. Not so the Floating Market, already a highly commercialised tourist trap.

Sometimes our wanderings took us into areas of filth and poverty. I remember one where all the worn out motorbikes in Thailand seemed to be undergoing repair, but even there we suddenly came on another temple glittering like a delicious trinket above the dirt.

Much of the waterfront on the great Menam river then consisted of go-downs ... old warehouses, and wooden Thai buildings, but now they are gone, and a mass of concrete and new hotels stand in their place. Gone too are many of the klongs down which breezes could sweep and cool the city, and which syphoned off flood water during the rains. The Oriental has doubled in size with a vast new wing dwarfing the lovely old building, and overshadowing the equally lovely French Embassy next door. I remember Kurt saying when this was first projected 'I can't think how they expect me to fill 260 more rooms!' In fact they are never empty; such is the style and reputation of the Oriental. But for several years more I was able to enjoy the beauty of the old Menam suite overlooking the river.

In the 1970s the Weekend Market still took place on the wide Pranam, open ground beside the Royal Palace. It was an endless source of delight. The orchid market was spectacular and stretched for quarter of a mile. Not normally an orchid-fan ... they look too unreal ... I found the profusion of colour and variety quite lovely. There were also stalls for everything, from tropical fruits, spices, and food of every colour, to fighting fish and animals. I never went near the latter, they looked so pathetic in the heat as they awaited goodness knows what fate ... But it is the people's market, and one must accept their customs. Now it has moved out into the suburbs and many of the old style traders have ceased to come.

During my first visit we spent a week at Pattaya on the gulf of Siam; ... but never again. It was already spoilt from being a rest camp for American troops during the Viet Nam war. The sea was muddy and shallow, but our hotel had a large and lovely garden, and what joy! ... a baby elephant lived there. We discovered it one morning in a clearing, eating a rather dull lunch of branches. It was quite big but still had a bristly fuzz of brown baby hair on its head and all down its spine. I rushed back to our room and collected all the fruit we had not been able to finish at breakfast. The elephant was enchanted with this and we with it. Thereafter I went every morning to see it and got such a welcome. The young mahout who looked after it was equally beautiful, and it was learning to be with people, but I never saw anyone else there. They went down to another hotel most afternoons, sauntering along the beach. I had a very pretty batik skirt ... red, with ceremonial elephants printed all round it and up the front which I had got in Sri Lanka, and Sylvia took some 'fun' photographs of me talking to the elephant and wearing this skirt. Sometimes it ate its lunch sitting down like a dog on its behind, and if one wanted to climb on it obligingly stuck out one hip as a step, while continuing to munch.

In the years that followed I went often to Thailand. The watercolours which I painted of it sold exceptionally well even to people who had never been there, due I am sure to the charm and beauty of the subjects. In those early days it cost under £300, all in, for two weeks; now it is nearer £2,000. The small shops and stalls open to the street are giving way to concrete shopping centres, and Westernisation is removing much of the individuality and charm.

Hua Hin on the East coast of the Siam peninsular became my favourite seaside place. It is more than a hundred miles from Bangkok and was then

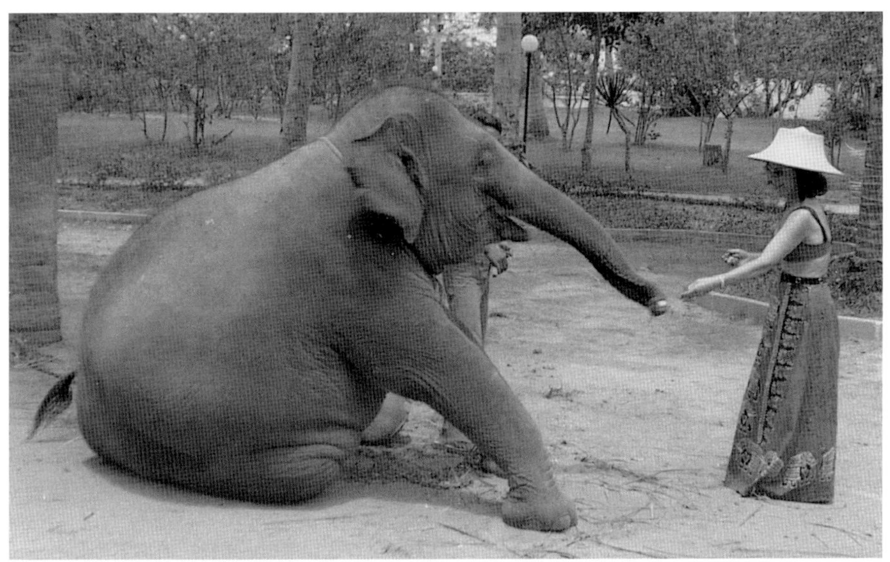

Lydia feeding the charming young elephant in the garden

an unspoilt fishing port, with a small factory where pretty Thai girls in white caps and overalls pushed masses of squid, starfish, and other little fish through mangles; after which they were spread like lace on wire trays to dry in the sun.

Hua Hin had been a favourite overnight stopping place too for people travelling down by train from the great teak forests in the North to trade in Malaya and Singapore, so there was a fine old railway hotel by the sea, with lovely gardens. It lay half a mile from the station, but one bowled down in tricycle rickshaws. It was very popular with my more discerning friends some of whom had Thai wives, and the food was delicious. Though shabby then it had so much charm, including all the old Royal Thai Railway china.

The King of Thailand had a small palace there and had built an excellent golf course. Two new hotels had been built a few miles away where I also stayed ... and the old Railway Hotel has now been completely refurbished without losing any of its graceful appearance. Much of the old teak panelling has been reused or copied, the lotus lamps, and the china being still on view. But I wonder if the same little herd of cows and calves wearing tinkling bells still walks past along the beach at twilight on its way home to be milked? I hope it does.

There was a big old wooden summer palace some miles up the beach from Cha Am, surrounded by huge Frangipani trees with their white waxy flowers and wonderful scent. It seemed deserted except for a few peacocks, and a police post not far off. I walked there one evening with two friends and loved its dreaming, timeless atmosphere.

In six or seven visits I saw so much of this lovely country that I can only mention bits of it. The ancient ruined cities further North like Sukhothai and Sri Satchanalai have the same magical dreamlike quality. Lampoon has the most beautiful temple of all, very old, but still in use with high gilded towers ... chedis ... and teak carved like lace over glittering turquoise glass. The country there is lush and lavishly farmed; everywhere one comes across unexpected treats like a man driving a huge flock of ducks along a road; they all stopped and moved to one side at a word of command from him to let us pass.

Of course one saw bad things too, the diseased and starving dogs, lepers, and overworked women. The good and the bad so often go together. One side of Thailand which I never saw was the famous nightlife of Pat Pong. The Minister of Tourism was taking Sylvia and me there one evening when I had a spectacular fainting fit at dinner beforehand, eating lobster bisque soup which I adore, so had to be taken home instead. I dread these faints which have dogged me for years, always afraid that people will think it is due to drugs or drink, especially there, when it is really exhaustion and lack of air. In fact I expect Pat Pong was no great loss ... rather degrading, especially for women. We did sometimes see pale tired little Thai call-girls out with big beefy western men twice their size, and gathered that most of them were trying hard to earn enough money to retire and get married so that they could return to their villages.

Some girls were sensational looking. One morning when the Museum was closed a Thai friend arranged for me to sketch and photograph three of them there ... actresses ... wearing 16th century clothes of glorious silk. This was rewarding but expensive, as they had to hire the clothes, but I later painted large pictures of them which are amongst my best work, still unsold, as seldom exhibited, and unappreciated here. The colours of the silks are indescribable. They owe much to an American called Jim Thompson who was in Thailand and Burma during the war, and later set about revitalizing the silk industry which was in a bad state of decline. He discovered permanent dyes and lovely traditional designs which made a fortune for him and the silk trade. He himself disappeared in extraordinary circumstances about 1978 while staying with Chinese (I think) friends Dr and Mrs. Ling at their country house in the Cameron Highlands, Malaya. He went out for a walk after lunch one day and has never been seen since. A tremendous search was made with tracer dogs and aeroplanes, but nothing was ever found, not even trampled grass. His old Thai house in Bangkok is now a museum, and the table is laid for dinner as it always was, in case he returns. A true Thai mystery.

For some years I avoided the River Kwai, partly repelled by the ridiculous film of that name (made in Ceylon) about the big wooden railway bridge, but more because of the dreadful suffering and deaths that took place there amongst the Allied Prisoners of the Japanese during the second world war. Then, weak with starvation and disease, they were beaten and tortured into building the railway up and into Burma, in temperatures often near 100 degrees Fahrenheit. One of those who survived is my friend and neighbour, Jim Rea here in Ireland, later to become President of the Singapore City Council. He told me the river country was in fact very beautiful; so, attracted by the raft and river life, I went with two friends. At that time it was little commercialised and we stayed near NamTok at the River Kwai Village hotel, then the only one, with marvellous food, and simple huts to sleep in.

Many people have now visited the bridge ... a metal one, not the historic wooden one built by the prisoners which has long since disappeared; so I will only say that the wide sweep of the river there in no way resembles that in the film. The graveyard of the prisoners was unspeakably sad ... many were so young, eighteen to twenty years; and thousands of European bodies were never found: none at all of the enormous number of Asian slave labourers who died there too. Having read the books written by some of the survivors I could not bring myself to go into the little museum on the river bank to see the photographs and memorabilia, but my friends did and said it was both well and movingly done.

There is a Buddhist temple nearby, so I sat there in the shade and watched three men, Thais, who were eating something wrapped is a very big leaf. They offered me some to taste and it turned out to be fermented rice ... interesting, but not recommended! I bought a little bamboo owl for Jim, and another for myself to remind me that however bad life may seem at times, it is unlikely ever to be as bad as his once was, there.

Our village was some thirty miles further on up the river. It lies in a wide gorge with high sides clothed in thick jungle. Being limestone country, in the dry season the water is a deep emerald green with lovely reflections, except where it rippled over shallows. The first morning we set off upstream in a long-tailed boat to the Nam Tok waterfall some miles away. It was glorious on the water and each curve and bend of the river brought us another lovely view, until we could see the Burma mountains, pale blue, in the distance. Many kingfishers and water birds darted about the banks. Water buffalo and even an elephant had been brought down to bathe; but the prettiest things to me were the little raft houses. These were moored to the bank, sometimes alone, sometimes in groups, made of bamboo with steep thatched roofs and floating on their platforms of bamboo which stuck out some way on either side. We stopped at one of them to eat our picnic lunch and enjoy the river people's life. After lunch we swam to the waterfall and splashed about in the cool clear water. I could not help thinking what a marvellous pot for my long handled paint brushes a nice length of bamboo would be ... each joint is sealed; so I swam down the rafts till I found one with a man chopping kindling. I then did a pantomime of sawing off a piece of his raft. He thought I wanted a lifebelt and produced a rubber tyre! So I clambered out and gave a demonstration. Only slightly surprised, he got a saw and politely cut off a piece of raft for me. Wreathed in smiles of success I swam back upstream to our boat with the bamboo under my chin feeling rather like a Labrador retriever. There was quite a strong current so one needed both hands to swim. After collecting a ten baht note I swam down again. This he firmly waved aside indicating that he was only too pleased to give me a piece of his house. So back I went once more with the note in my mouth and got a biro pen, swam down again, and it was received with happy smiles.

This was all great fun, and when I returned to Bangkok a friend there carved 'Lydia, the River Kwai 1984' on my pot, in Thai. At least I hope that is what he carved! And I use it every day painting.

Next morning we boated downstream to Lum Sum[1] past the great Wam Po viaduct built by the prisoners and still standing strong and proud. We meant to catch the train back to Nam Tok but it was hours late. Lum Sum consists of one wooden bungalow with a veranda where the train stops. We got awfully hungry waiting and the kind owners took pity on us and shared their lunch with us. It seemed to consist of pink, green and white noodles and was most welcome. There was only one train a day and the railway is no longer in use above Nam Tok, but being high up the views are quite lovely, and a resident friend told me later that one of the nicest things to do in the cool season was to walk the railway even further up.

There could not be a more delightful way of spending a few days than living in one of those raft houses. After the rains of course the river is in flood and it would be too dangerous.

---

[1] I gather many of the place names, including those along the railway where the prisoners were camped have since been changed.

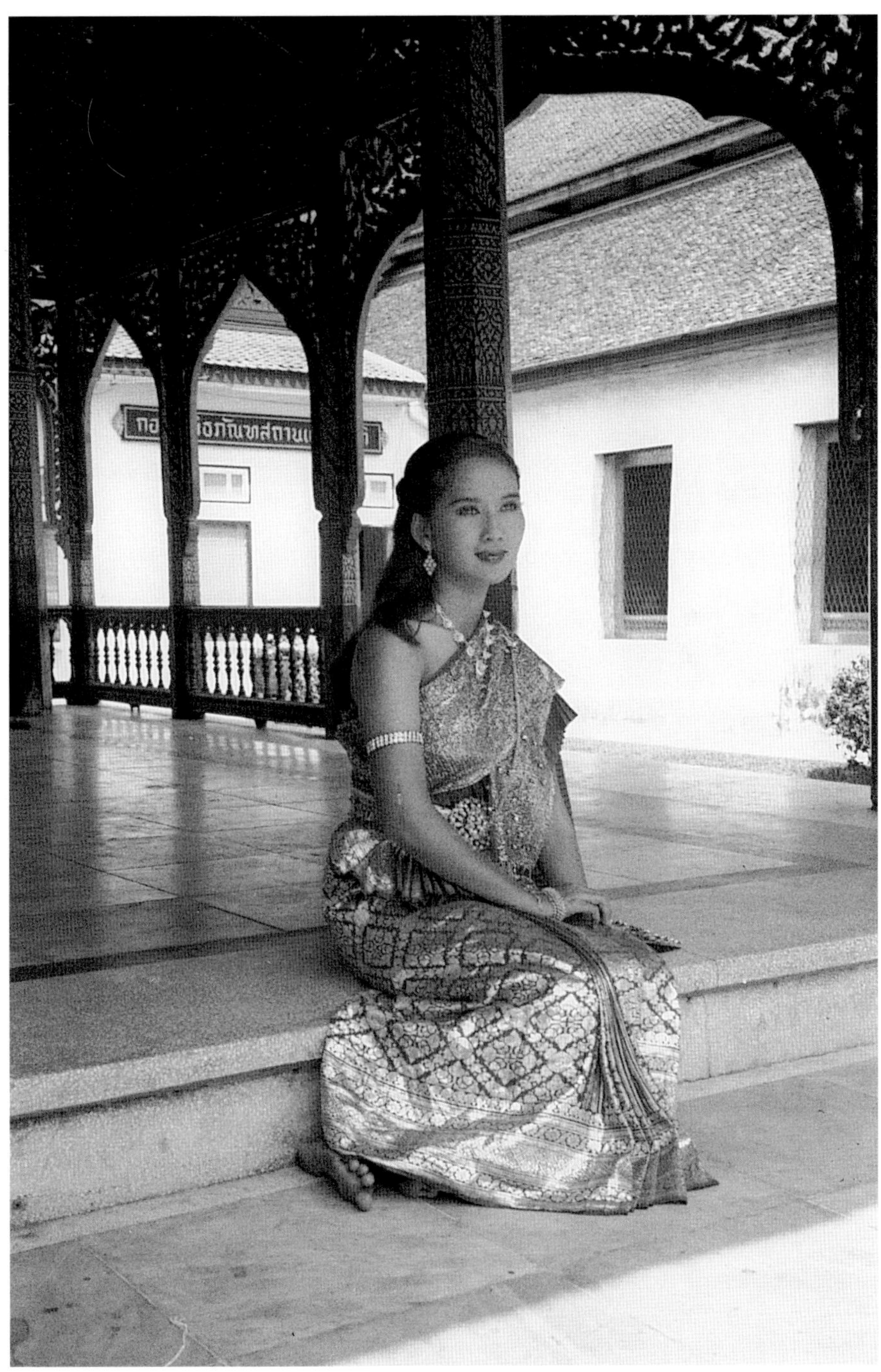

Thai actress modelling for Lydia, Bangkok Museum

CHAPTER 2

THE CAMPBELLS

MY MOTHER'S FAMILY

LOVE OF TRAVEL seems to stem from my earliest days. It is not so much the travelling itself as the lure of discovery that beckons; beautiful things to see and do, to smell and eat; magical countries and people beyond even my fertile imagination.

In 1926 when I was three my father was a Commander in the Royal Navy, so my early life was spent travelling.

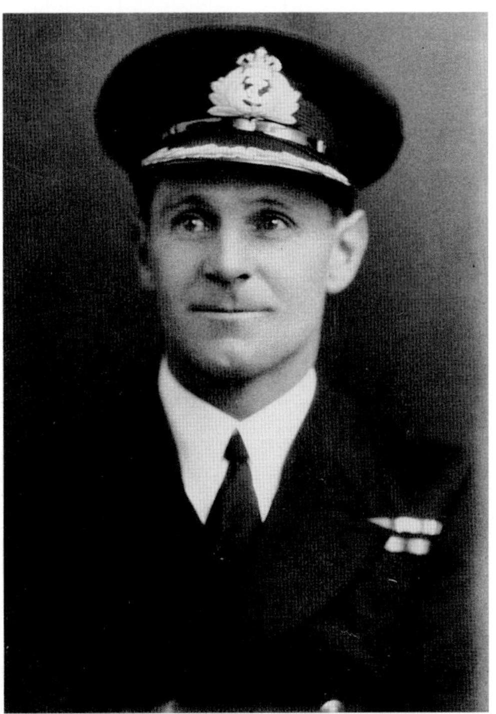

My father, Commander Charles de Burgh, D.S.O. 1922

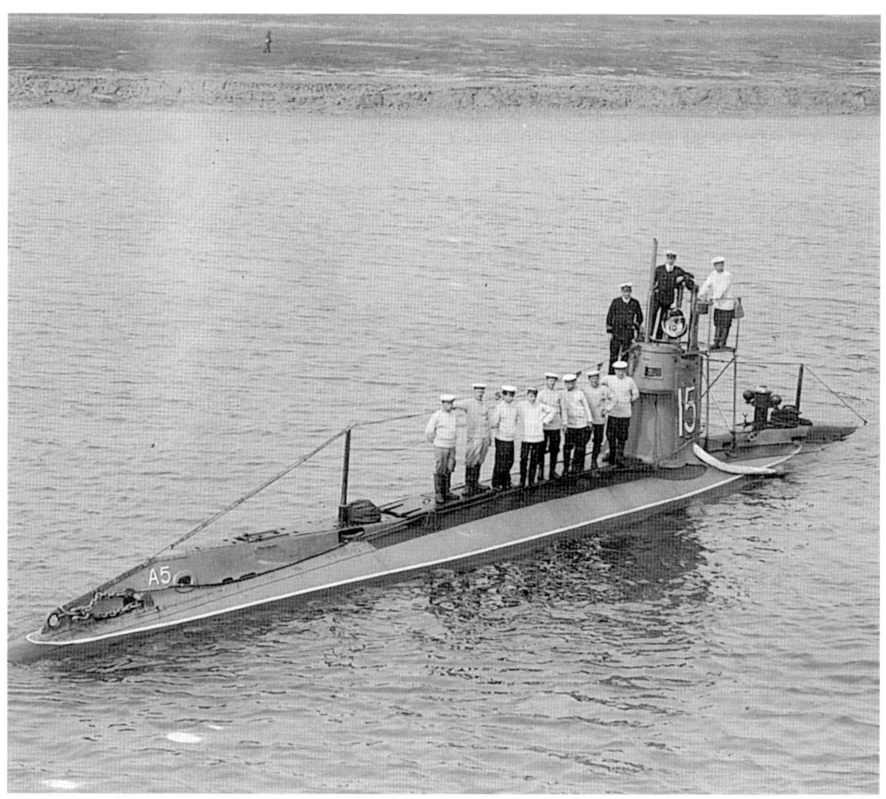

H.M. Submarine A5, 1908 – my father on the conning tower

Originally a pioneer submariner, he was now doing 'big ship' time in the Mediterranean and elsewhere whither my mother accompanied or followed him. Having been married for nearly fourteen years before we children were born she had no intention of giving this up, even when it meant trailing my infant sister and me, Nanny, and vast quantities of luggage. Having five brothers and four de Burgh brothers-in -law she was bored rigid with other women.

We travelled by whatever transport was available, trains and steamers, cattle boats and mule carts. When based at Nice and St. Jean de Luz we could drive in my father's battered Armstrong Siddeley which he took with him on board HM Ships Cyclops and Valiant. In this way we had wandered all round the Mediterranean by the time I was four, and I loved it. I am not sure my mother did, but she loved my father so wanted to be with him.

Abroad in the '20s and '30s of this century was far cheaper than living at home and we had very little money but my father's pay. Both my parents spoke French fluently, and I think one reason why my spelling is so bad is that we learnt French and English together; I always spell family and niece the French way. My mother loved France, the country, the food, the way of life and the people, and must have passed this on to me.

After 1936 it was twelve long years, six of them the war, before I travelled again, and then only spasmodically when I could afford to. So before launching into further journeys and adventures, and for the benefit of those who have not read 'Lydia's Story' I must revert to my childhood.

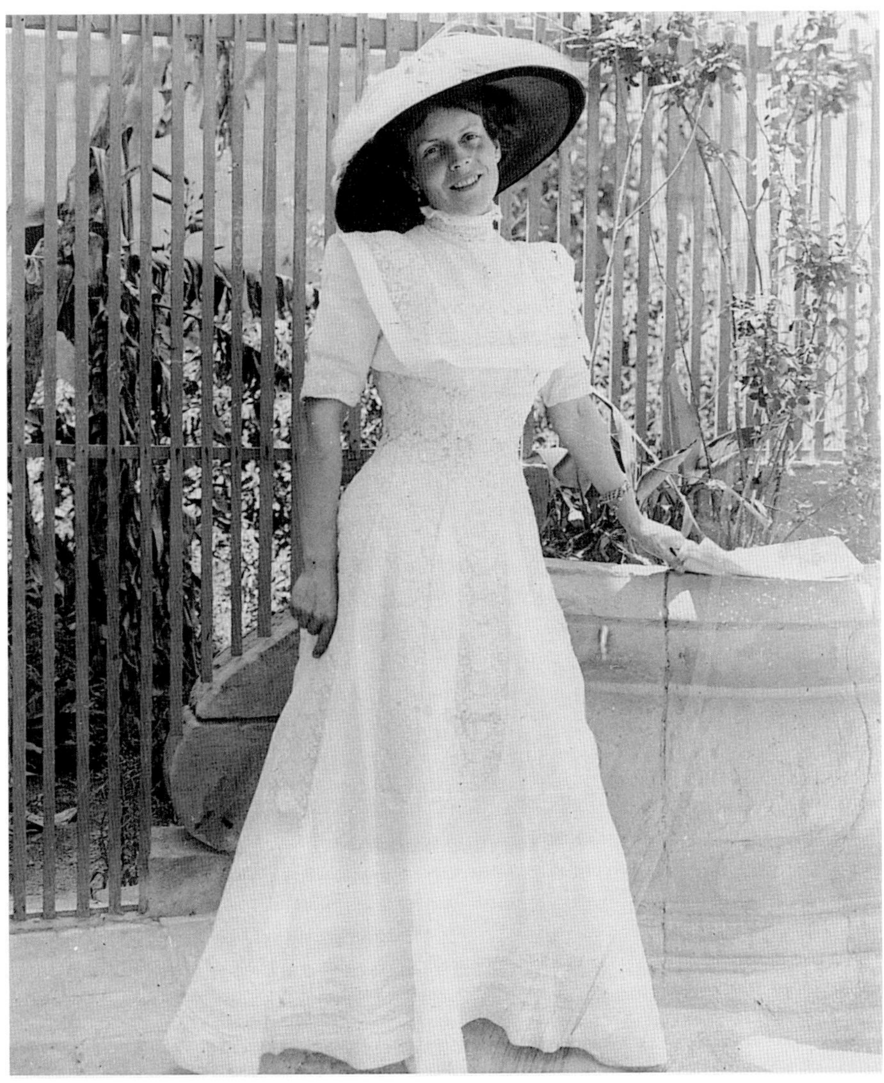

My mother, Isabel de Burgh, née Campbell, in Malta 1910

My mother's grandfather was born in 1797, eight years before Nelson won the battle of Trafalgar and four years after the execution of Queen Marie Antoinette in the French Revolution. It is now 1993, so only four generations of her family span nearly two hundred years. Perhaps that is why I have such a strong sense of history and enjoy it so much. The people and events of time long gone appear upon my inward eye as vividly as those today, often with more fascination.

My own personal recollections have already been recorded in 'Lydia's Story', but there are many other delightful snippets which filtered through from listening to my parents, their friends and relations talking of the past, while as a child I played some game behind the drawingroom sofa. Their voices were clear, charming and gentle, with no trace of affectation, no swearing and of course no slang! I dare not think what they would feel about the more graphic way I often talk today, but I was taught how to express myself; and when not to!

Irish country house life and schooldays did not drastically change until after the second world war. Most people in big houses were chronically and continually short of money, but Victorian thrift was luckily still the fashion and 'waste not, want not' the order of the day. My mother could remember learning as a small child this doggerel:

'Dearly beloved brethren, pray is it not a sin
To eat a good potato and throw away the skin,
For skins feed pigs, and pigs feed you;
Dearly beloved brethren is this not true?'

Once when Uncle Morris Campbell aged ten was coming home from his preparatory school for the holidays my grandmother had sent him some pocket money for the journey. Alas, by the time he had to change trains at Portadown for Dungannon on the last lap all but one halfpenny had been spent. Unabashed and with a lordly air he tipped the porter who had loaded his luggage into the train with the halfpenny; and the porter was so furious he took all the luggage out again and dumped it on the platform.

At that time my mother's father the Rev. Edward Fitzharding Campbell, son of the Dean of Dromore, was Rector of Killyman in Co. Tyrone. He had married Lydia Morris the youngest daughter of a lawyer who lived in Bengorm Place, a big house (now demolished) in Lurgan. When she was born her eldest sister was already married, which explains why the family became so extended. Lydia's mother had been orphaned by the great cholera epidemic which swept Ireland in 1830, and which they tried to avoid by fleeing to Warrenpoint. But others had done the same bringing the fatal disease with them. Both her parents died, and she was made a Ward of Court.

Killyman was a small but lively parish. My grandfather was a considerable scholar and had many other commitments; amongst these he was Chairman for the Lord Enniskillen Memorial Fund for Orphans, and Grand Chaplain of the Orange Order. He also loved fishing especially on Lough Melvin where they rented a small lodge. He and my grandmother had seven children, so with five of them sons to be educated they were not at all well off. Fortunately my grandmother had some money of her own so they managed well enough.

In those days my grandfather went once a fortnight at least by train, to the Ulster Club in Belfast, where men of standing forgathered – including politicians, lawyers, clergy and landowners, which kept them in touch so well with what was going on. He also went to Dublin in the same way, though less often, and of course to Armagh. I expect my grandmother sometimes went too, driven to the station by Billy the gardener in the pony and trap.

Sad to say nearly all the lovely houses and old families near Killyman which they used to visit have now ceased to exist; the Verners at Verners Bridge, the Moutrays at Favour Royal, the Burgeses at Parkanaur, the Charlemonts at Roxborough Castle, McGeogh-Bonds at the Argory and many more. Of most houses not a stone remains. By the time I was eighteen only Parkanaur, where I often stayed, and the Argory were still private houses.

Visiting one hundred years ago was limited to what could be done with a horse and carriage; but I am sure the conversation was good, and of course music was very important. All ladies played the piano, the harp, or sang; so did many of the men. Talent was eagerly sought, and social life flourished.

Many years later in 1950 when I was staying with the Burgeses I took part in what was perhaps the last faint echo of such evening parties, at Ecclesville near Fintonagh, the home of Raymond Browne-Lecky. We were all invited to this 'soirée'. Alfred Burges himself recited rather well, very amusing doggerels which he wrote in his bath ... we all wrote them; it was great fun. I cannot remember whether he was performing that night but he had certainly told Raymond that I was training as an opera singer and I was co-opted on to the programme. Raymond, known generally as 'Tibby', was himself an excellent pianist, though rather old. I sang 'Deh Vieni' from the Marriage of Figaro, and 'Goin' Home' from the New World Symphony, all dressed up in a white tulle ball-gown (actually my bridesmaid's dress from my sister's wedding) and standing under a huge glittering chandelier. Other renderings were given by the local talent with varying degrees of success, and if only I had not been so frightened ... and so cold! It would have been really hilarious, a perfect capsule of life before the 1914 war. Everyone of course was wearing full evening dress.

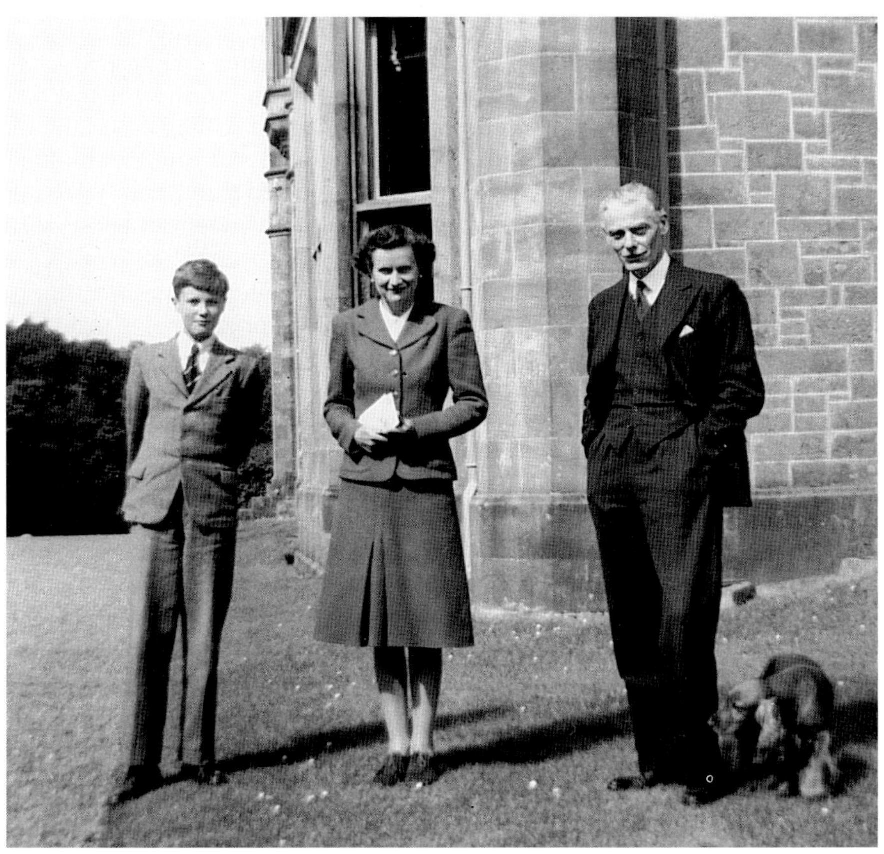

Major and Mrs Alfred Burges and son Michael, Parkanaur, 1949

It was snowing as we were leaving, and ,clutching our coats or furs around us we were slightly taken aback when a piping hot mince pie was put into each person's hand. It was a charming thought, but our hands were so cold and the pies were so hot we kept dropping them and bits of pie and pastry flew in all directions.

I thought no more about all this until two days later at breakfast Alfred started to read out of the 'Dungannon Courier' or something a high-flown account of the soirée in pure Victorian language. I thought he was making the whole thing up to amuse me ... he could well have done so, but no! There word for word was the following:

> *'CHRISTMAS PARTY AT ECCLESVILLE'*
>
> *Since Mr. Lecky-Browne-Lecky's return to Ecclesville he has made a feature of giving pleasure to a wide circle of friends, and*

we think that the Musical Party that he gave on Wed. Dec. 15th was the most brilliant yet. Certainly from the standpoint of culture this was the most delightful treat, and Mr. Browne-Lecky entertained upwards of 120 guests ... The spacious rooms with beautiful floral arrangements were very much admired by all. Great interest was aroused by the first appearance in Ireland (sic) of the lovely young professional singer Lydia de Burgh who is at present staying as the guest of Major and Mrs. Burges.

The programme started with a pianoforte solo, Sibelius' 'Finlandia' by the host Mr Browne-Lecky. Mrs Garland of Corick was in fine voice and her solos were much enjoyed. Oliver Welsh, the well known Omagh singer delighted the audience with his songs.

Lydia de Burgh sang an Italian aria and several songs, much to the delight of everyone. Special praise is due to Isabel Bryson (Mrs. Rainey) whose singing of Hamilton Harty's 'Sweetheart' was very fine. The accompaniments were played by Mrs. Irvine, Mrs. Walsh and Miss Joan Story and the rendering was delightful.

The catering for the tea was carried out by that well-known Omagh firm, the Cake Shop, and left nothing to be desired.

A feature at the conclusion of the party was the handing round of hot mince pies to every guest as a good wish for Christmas and the New Year.

I cut this gem out and stuck it in my album and see I have written underneath: 'Oh my! Pie in the eye!'

Very old newspapers in fact fascinate me. There was so much to read, wonderful descriptions of social events from Balls to race meetings: who was there and what they wore. Huge lists of wedding presents were described in detail; and much more. Imagine the vision conjured up by 'Mrs Snodgrass wore purple satin trimmed with ruffled lace, and a diamond aigrette and stomacher (whatever that was?) Her train was of lilac crepe and she carried an ostrich feather fan.' These descriptions went on for columns and were absolutely addictive! Alas what would the guests today sound like ... Lord S. would be wearing a dung coloured Barbour and gum-boots ... 'wellies,' Mrs Snodgrass would be in tight jeans and a see-through shirt; and everybody else would look almost the same.

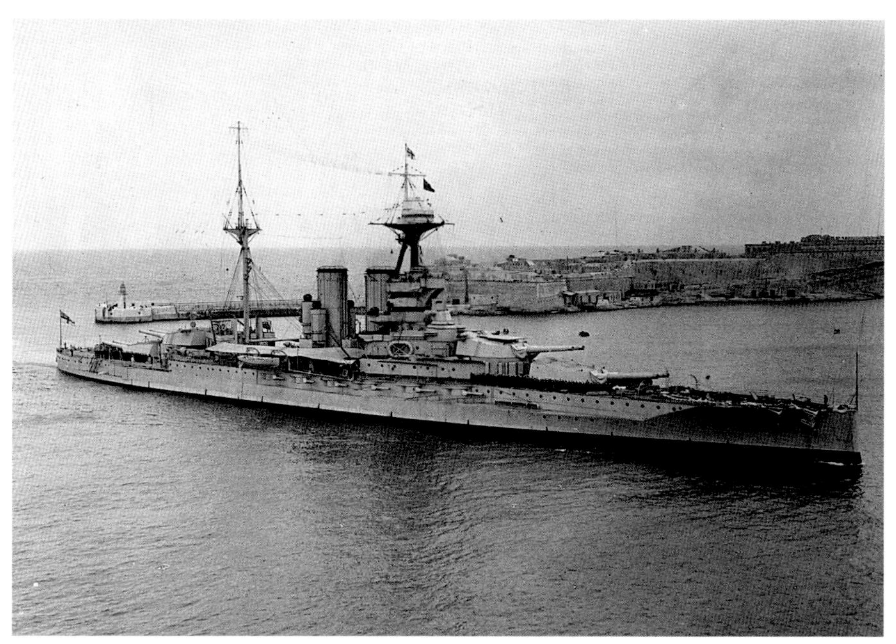

H.M.S. Valiant, Malta 1926–27

CHAPTER 3

BALLYCASTLE

MY PARENTS WERE MARRIED at Killyman in 1910, and my grandparents were still there in the big old rectory when war broke out in 1914. With four sons and a son-in-law ... my father ... already in the Royal Navy and the Army they must have had a most anxious war.

The first upheaval however was in fact quite funny. Uncle Geoffrey was serving in the Royal Irish Fusiliers, and when they were ordered to the Front as soon as war broke out he dumped his entire private pack of foxhounds at the rectory to be housed and fed. Both Granny and my Aunt Jane were very feminine and could not bear dogs. The hounds were not only somewhat rough and rude but distinctly smelly as well, with healthy sexual appetites. I do not know how long this state of affairs lasted, but I can just imagine the tableau.

Having survived the retreat from Mons Uncle Geoffrey was then sent to Gallipoli, but his troopship was torpedoed on the way and this probably saved his life, because after hours in the sea nearly drowning he was rescued and returned home, and never got to Gallipoli where the casualties were appalling. Uncle Colin, my mother's favourite brother[1] died tragically with his wife and baby daughter when the mailboat, the Leinster, was torpedoed in the Irish channel by a German submarine on the 10th of October, 1918, and sank almost at once with great loss of life. They were returning to England from leave.

This was a dreadful blow to my poor grandparents; Granny and Uncle Colin had travelled down by train to Dublin the day before, and 'we had such a lovely, lovely talk', she wrote later, little knowing it would be their last. Aunt Eileen and baby Betty had gone there the day before to shop. All the bodies were washed up later and poor grandfather had to identify theirs. Uncle Colin, a Lieutenant Commander in the Royal Navy, had tar

---

[1] Uncle Colin, together with Professor Bennet, invented the Campbell-Bennet deadbeat periodic compass, which first made blind flying possible, and which he tested flying himself.

on his sleeve and they thought he might have been trying to throw a rope. I still have letters the family wrote to each other at that sad time with the war so nearly over, and I still wear the signet ring with a boar's head on it that Uncle Colin was wearing that night.

My parents were married for over fourteen years before having any children; not from choice, but what with the war, my father's long spells away at sea, and ill health, Coralie and I did not appear upon the scene till the 1920s. I am the elder by one year, and we could not possibly have had better parents about whom I have already written much elsewhere.

I was five when my grandparents moved to Ballycastle on the Antrim coast and rented an old house called Sheskburn, facing the tennis courts. Ballycastle in 1928 was a charming little town, very popular with retired people and for holidays. Besides the fishing port it had once had flourishing soap and glass factories, and much of the town belonged to the Boyd family. There was a good golf course, and excellent tennis courts the foundations of which were the packed sand which had once been the inner harbour. The Ballycastle tennis tournaments were a great feature of social life, with people coming from all over Ulster. They still take place there in August now.

We loved staying at Sheskburn which was a four-storied house with a big coach yard at the back. There was no electricity so there were lots of lamps, stoves and candles, and good fires burned in many of the rooms. We children were never allowed to touch the lamps and had a healthy fear of fire which was always a very real danger. There was an Aladdin lamp on each newel post of the stairs, so a cosy smell of paraffin hung faintly on the air. Our nurseries were on the top floor, and lying in bed at night I loved to watch the flashing beam of the lighthouse on Rathlin Island three miles away. My sister slept like a top but I was often awake and the only thing that kept me in bed was fear that some monster was lurking underneath it to grab me by the legs.

Downstairs there was a big drawingroom, then seldom used, full of Victorian rosewood furniture ... spoonbacked chairs covered in flowery chintze. This was all shrouded in dust-sheets under which I loved to explore. Granny now spent most of her time in her little sittingroom, round which the household as it were revolved. At eighty she still had an excellent head for business and kept meticulous accounts. Grandfather's study was on the first floor where he was usually to be found surrounded by high shelves of leather-bound books, writing and reading in his big, buttoned, worn leather chair. He had a beautiful gold pocket watch which played a tune, and he always seemed so pleased to see us.

My sister and I loved the kitchen too but it seemed miles away down a long dark passage with sinister doors leading off it. We used to take a deep breath and run as fast as we could to the warmth and safety. I think the doors only hid pantries and larders but one never knew! (We were brought up to be brave and never show fear, but one often felt it!) In the kitchen were Elizabeth Humphrey the cook, Rose the housemaid, and Old Betty who had been nanny to my mother and her six brothers and sister, all as wild as hawks I suspect. Old Betty was now ninety, very frail and toothless in a long black dress and shawls, and spent most of her days in a basket chair by the fire of the big kitchen range. There was always a delicious smell of baking, and we loved sticking cherries on cakes with much licking of fingers.

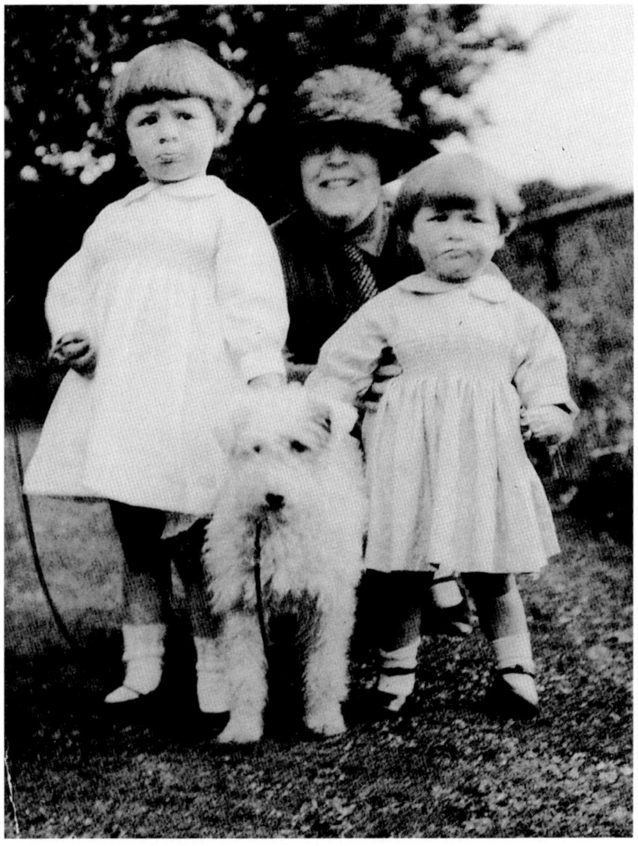

Lydia and Coralie de Burgh at Sheskburn with Mummy and 'Witty', 1927

In those days almost everyone had domestic staff, and although their wages were low they were fed, clothed and cared for and often their families as well. There was great poverty and little other employment;

tuberculosis was rife in Ireland, not only among the poor. No stigma was attached then to domestic service, and in big houses the protocol below stairs was far greater than that above.

All those years my grandparents and Aunt Jane worked hard to alleviate the distress of the poor. Aunt Jane also organised and produced excellent amateur theatricals for charity in the Ballycastle Orange Hall. At the age of six I sat entranced at 'The Country Girl' and the 'Chinese Honeymoon', charming musicals. Mr. McVicker(?) the chemist usually played and sang the male lead, debonair and accomplished, and everyone else with talent took part, from wardrobe to scenery.

Aunt Jane sometimes took me shopping with her, and I remember Mrs. McGarry who ran the butcher's shop down a steep hill from the Diamond. She was a small and birdlike woman with a rather red nose, it was always very cold in the little shop. This was no doubt good for the meat ... (there was ice of course, but no fridgidaires.) Great arguments took place about how long it had been hung. In those days meat, especially beef, was never killed at one year old and eaten fresh, tough and tasteless. It was hung for a week at least and was much darker and beautifully marbled with little veins of fat which dissolved when cooked and gave it such a wonderful rich juicy taste. The fat had to be very white and fresh, never yellow.

In the Manor House near Sheskburn lived the two Miss Boyds with whom my aunt often played Bridge, and further up the road were the two Misses Douglas with curled fringes like Queen Alexandra. One of these was still alive when I returned to Ballycastle in 1946 after the war for the tennis tournament, and I was sent to stay as a paying guest with her.

Alas, I soon fell from grace. Dick Musgrave, now Sir Richard, and Duncan Wauchope ... now dead, were my partners at tennis. One evening they took me out rowing in a small boat after dinner. The wind got up, an oar broke and was lost, and we had the most awful job getting back against the tide. Cold, frightened and exhausted, the boys escorted me back to Miss Douglas. It was midnight, but she was standing on the doorstep in her dressing-gown in a towering rage. How dare I disgrace her house by coming back at that hour, and looking like a tramp! She fairly took us apart, and practically accused me of being a 'fallen woman'.

'Oh I say, Miss Douglas' expostulated Dick, 'I would have you know my Colonel in India always entrusted his daughters to me only to bring them home from parties!'

'Huh, huh,' muttered Duncan, not helping matters, 'I think I'd consider that rather an insult!' By this time I was reduced to tears of exhaustion, and Miss D. flatly refused to let them drive me home to Conway next day.

But she had reckoned without Auntie, who rang up as soon as I returned and fairly thundered at her. How dare she imply that her niece was lying, or improper in any way! These young men were impeccable, and she ought to be ashamed of herself! Miss Douglas was well and truly pulverised and honour was saved! What a vast gap in generations there was then, I was twenty three, and we had all three just served through a dreadful war.

The only other family I remember as a child at Ballycastle were the Boylans. To Dr. Boylan we were especially indebted because he saved my mother's life when she was desperately ill in 1930.

There were always other children about so we did not lack company then on our visits.

Often their parents were serving abroad in Egypt or India, climates not good for children, and they had been parked with their grandparents for the holidays. We used to go for long walks in the lovely country round about with our governess. On fine days we took a picnic and had a treasure hunt. The 'treasure' consisted of Playmate biscuits, which had a hard coating of brown icing on one side embellished with figures in white. They tasted in fact like sawdust, I thought, but the excitement was in finding them.

Our pocket money consisted of two pence a week, old pence that is ... slightly less than one and a half new pence. This was really quite enough because one could buy for two pence quite a large bag of sweets and we were never allowed more than one sweet a day. Bullseyes and butterscotch were considered best as chocolate cost much more, but what I had a secret passion for was sherbet. One could buy a triangular packet of sherbet with a stick of liquorice in it for a halfpenny. One dipped the stick in the sherbet and licked it off; I loved the way it fizzled on my tongue. But it was not considered suitable; it made us burp and smell of licorice so could only be indulged in rarely and surreptitiously!

Sad to say when I was last in Ballycastle, seven years ago, not a stone of Sheskburn remained except a tiny corner of the yard wall. In its place was a huge concrete coeducational school. Now I believe that too is going; but the good tennis courts remain, and so does the flashing lighthouse on Rathlin Island which I had watched from my little bed over sixty years before.

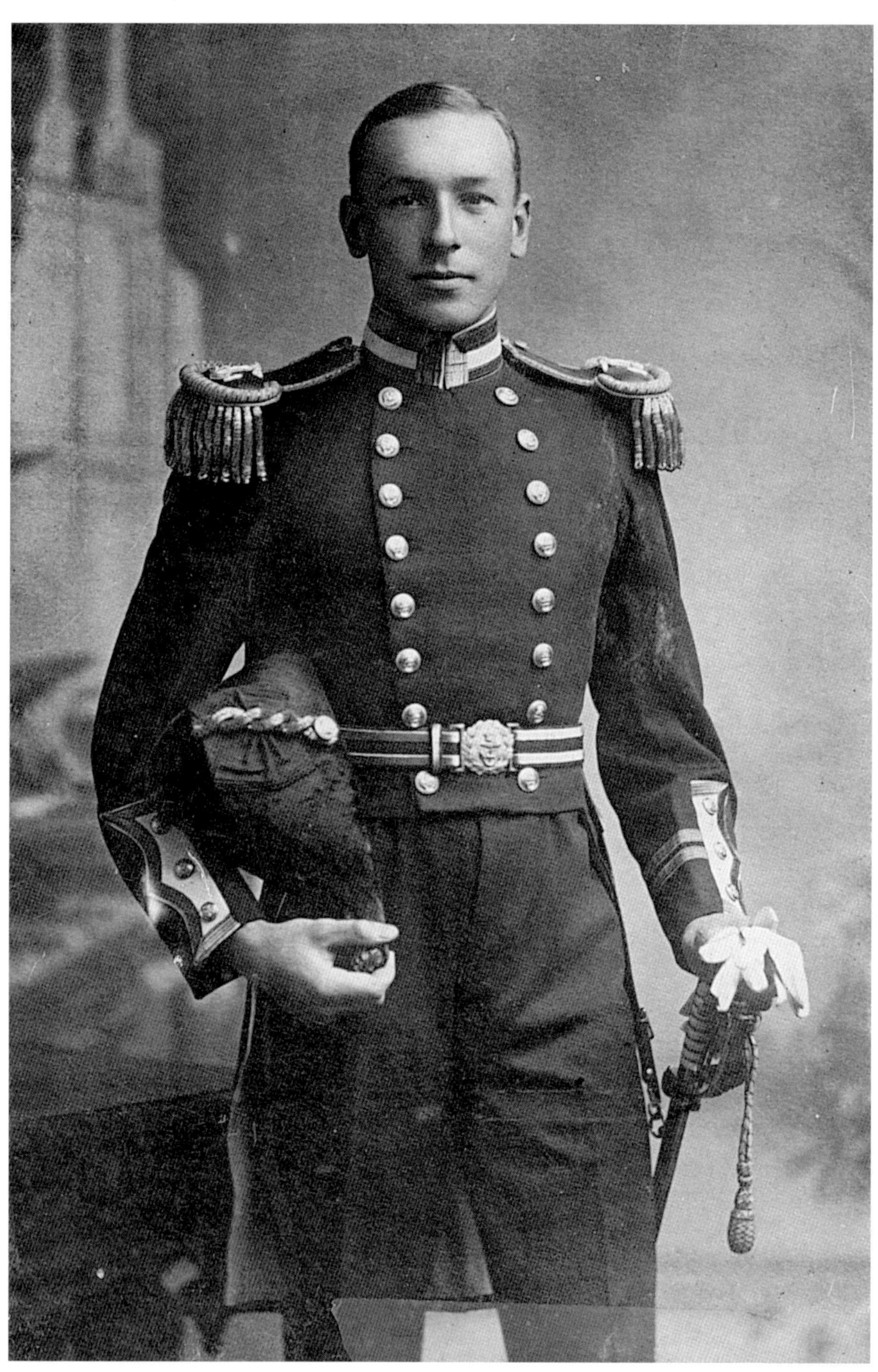

Uncle Colin Campbell, R.N.

CHAPTER 4

MY FATHER'S FAMILY

THE SAGA OF THE de Burghs in Ireland begins in 1172.

Before that Richard Earl of Pembroke known as Strongbow came to Ireland at the behest of Dermot McMorrough, who promised his daughter Eva and much land for help against his enemy Tiernan O'Ruarie and his Leinster rebels.[1] The first knights and army arrived in 1169, followed by Strongbow and his bride Eva who landed at Waterford with a thousand men.

When Dermot died Strongbow became King of Leinster, and after visiting Ireland in 1171 King Henry II made his son John 'Dominus Hiberniae', and devolved the care of Ireland on him. Prince John came to Ireland aged nineteen in 1185 with a considerable army, and among his close friends were three young men of Norman descent destined to found great families in Ireland.

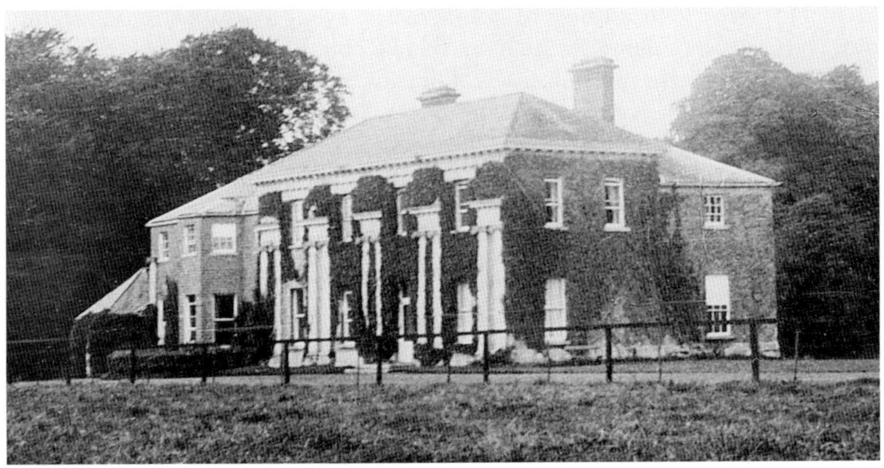

Oldtown, front view 1932. The original 1700 plan was never finished

[1] See 'History of the de Burgos', Burke's Landed Gentry of Ireland, and family records etc.

One of these was Sir William de Burgo from whom my family directly descends. He married the daughter of Donal More O'Brien of Munster having been given great fiefs of land, and the de Burghs or de Burgos, have been interwoven with Irish history ever since in many different ways, most if not all of them good.

My father's family, the de Burghs of Oldtown, live near Naas in County Kildare. Generations of them were members of parliament, and Thomas (de) Burgh was Surveyor General of Ireland, M.P. for Naas, and the architect of Trinity College Library, the old Custom House, Collins Barracks and Dr. Steevens Hospital, also of St. Mary's Church which is now the only 17th Century church left in Dublin. He built Oldtown House around 1703, but the original plan was never completed, due no doubt to the usual shortage of money. Like Russborough and many other Irish houses, it was meant to have two classical wings linked to a larger central block, but the central block was never built, only the two wings. (As one of these was the stables perhaps he had his priorities right!) Later, an ugly Victorian wing running back at right angles was added instead. This house was accidentally burnt in the 1950s, the classical house was destroyed and the Victorian kitchen wing needless to say survived. My cousin John pulled this down, restored the wing, which had been the stables, as the new house, and turned the whole place into a highly successful stud farm. The family still live at Oldtown today.

Grandfather, Colonel T. J. de Burgh J.P., D.L., was told at the early age of twenty seven that he had only six months to live, so he left the army. Finding himself still in excellent health much later, he managed somehow to take part in almost every war and skirmish thereafter, as I believe, a dispatch rider ... on a horse of course ... or even, like Winston Churchill, as a war correspondent. As such, at Tel el Kebir, his younger brother Ulick, a Captain in in the 3rd Dragoon Guards, was taking part in the great cavalry charge, when to his fury, he saw grandfather charging past him on his, Ulick's, best hunter, when he should not have been there at all![2]

Back in the army, Grandfather served throughout the South African war commanding the 17th Imperial Yeomanry and the 5th Dragoons; and again aged 65 in the 1914–18 war with a St John's Ambulance Unit. There he saved the life of a young friend Brian Bellew of Barmeath,[3] Co Louth, whom he found bleeding to death unattended in a Field dressing-station, and who many years later told me about it.

Like many de Burghs Grandfather had a passion for exercise, and apparently decided in 1910, being unable to hunt due to an injury, that he could not stand a family Christmas at home. He arranged to bicycle out to

---

[2] See 'Charmed Circle' by Liegh Maxwell.

[3] Later Lord Bellew.

stay with my newly married parents in Malta, despite a brother-in-law trying to tempt him to remain:

'I say Tom, don't go off to that country (France) where they don't even speak English. Come and ferret the big bank at Punchestown with me on Monday!' (Punchestown then belonged to Granny de Burgh's father the Baron de Robeck).

Eschewing all such attractions he set off alone ... bikes were still quite smart and new-fangled. He got to Malta via France, Italy and several boat journeys, stopping off at various watering holes en route where he invariably seems to have come across friends also avoiding the Irish winter. He kept a meticulous diary with postcards of this expedition ... unfortunately rather dull ... which I only found after my father died so could not discover more information about it.

Grandfather had married Emily de Robeck, said to be the prettiest girl in Kildare, whose father, the Baron, was a famous Master of the Kildare Foxhounds for twenty five years. He had great difficulty in persuading her to marry him; his last proposal was in the hunting field, and she turned him down yet again.

Exasperated by this, he swore to her that he would ride to his death, and galloped off in a fury! The Kildare Hunt were then treated to the sight of Emily galloping after him, calling 'Tommy, Tommy, don't do it! I WILL marry you!' She did, and they had two daughters and five sons, of whom my father was the fourth.

His passion for exercise continued unabated and when his daughter Zoë was about to get married, her fiancé Tom Maxwell visited Oldtown. One night when it was nearly pitch dark Grandfather suggested to Tom that they go for a walk in the woods. The beech woods in the demesne were very beautiful. Off they went, Grandfather behaving as if it was broad daylight, Tom struggling behind bumping into trees and stumbling into ditches. Afterwards Grandfather confessed that he had always been frightened of losing his sight and being unable to walk in his beloved woods. So he had trained himself to do so in the dark, learning every path and bridge by heart.[4]

Sad to say Granny Emily died of cancer before I was born. She had made a rose garden outside his study, a pattern of flower-beds bordered with trimmed box. After her death he kept this up himself for many years, and I do just remember it. He died when I was seven so I scarcely knew him, but three charming letters still exist and give some idea of what he and Emily were like.

---

[4] Liegh Maxwell, letter to me.

In 1896 young Sidney de Burgh of Cowalla, Gin Gin in Western Australia, a cousin, was at school in England, far, far, from home, and was coming to stay at Oldtown for the holidays. So Grandfather wrote:

'Dear Sidney,

I was glad to hear that you will come to us at the end of July. I hope you will write and tell us how you come so that if any of our boys are coming over at that time you can join them. We shall be glad to make your acquaintance. Meanwhile as cash is sometimes short in mid-term I send you a small tip, enclosed.'

Then later, in Sept. 1896 from Granny Emily,:

'My dear Sidney,

We were very glad to hear of your safe arrival. Eric (her second son) ... had a piece of bad luck, just missing the train at Swindon. It was actually steaming out of the station as he drove up and he had to wait there three hours.[5]

We are all most flourishing but feel quite lonely without you all; I am really glad you enjoyed your time here; I assure you we one and all enjoyed having you. It was a good thing you summoned up the courage to face this numerous and formidable array of cousins ... When the date is settled for your return to Australia don't forget to write and tell us about it for we are very interested in your movements.

I hope your bed has grown longer during the holidays!

Your affectionate cousin, Emily de Burgh.'

Finally, one from grandfather to Sidney reads:

'Naawport, Cape Colony
May 1901, South Africa,

Dear Sidney,

Your letter has been pursuing me round two continents and has finally arrived! ... Eric was badly disappointed not to be accepted for the Yeomanry on account of his youth, but has settled down to work at home and farming very satisfactorily. Coralie and Emily are well, Charlie, (my father) is going into the

---

[5] The Eric of these letters, my uncle, joined the army and served in South Africa, then transferred to Hodson's Horse, a famous Indian cavalry regiment, and became in 1939 a full General and Chief of Staff in India. He was the grandfather of Chris de Burgh, the well known rock-singer and composer, and his brother Richard.
He also insisted when I knew him on always getting to all stations a good hour before the train was due!

Navy, Hubert is in the Flagship, the 'Renown', ... I have been out here since last April and have worked down through Portuguese Territory, Rhodesia, Cape Colony, Orange River Colony and Transvaal with the Battalion I command, the strength of which has varied from 800 to 190 mounted men ... when we have horses. We have had very hard and trying work, had a fair deal of fighting, trekked thousands of miles, and are now on our way South for home.

I am glad to hear you are on your own legs at Cowalla, no man who has not worked hard at something in his youth is ever worth anything. I saw a good deal of the Australian contingents out here and very fine fellows they are ... Please remember me to your father and Aunt Fanny. It is a long time since I saw them in Ceylon. I wish you every success and hope we shall see you home again sometime.

Yours very sincerely
T. J. de Burgh, Lt. Colonel.'

This keeping up with family ties, now so much neglected, resulted in the Sidney of those letters, by then a very old man, sending us most welcome food parcels during the last war, and after his death William his son continued to do so. I was so happy to have an opportunity of visiting them a few years ago, still flourishing on the same sheep station they had pioneered over one hundred and fifty years before, though much reduced in size.

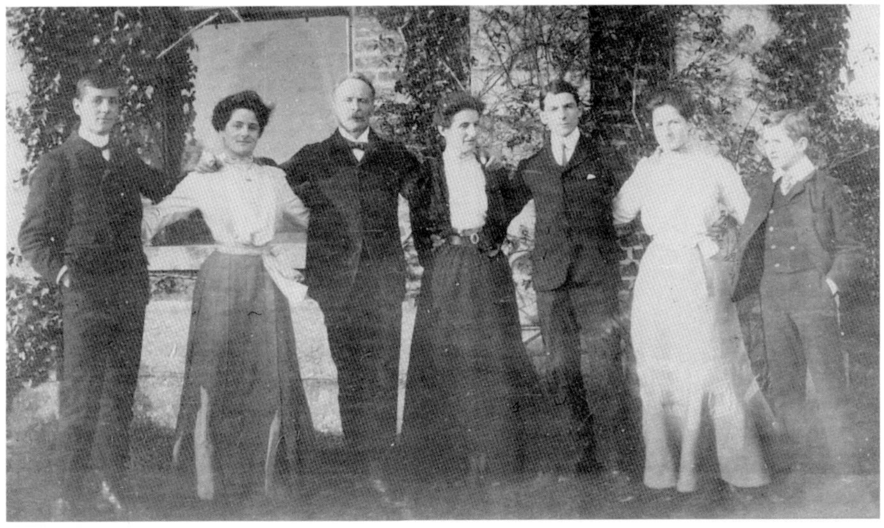

Some of the de Burghs at Oldtown, 1902
Charles, Coralie, Grandfather, Grandmother, Hubert, Zoë and Tommy

CHAPTER 5

CLOTHES AND CALLING

I MUST HAVE BEEN A STRANGELY clothes-conscious child even at the age of five because I can remember even then having strong likes and dislikes about what my parents and their friends wore. Women's clothes had of course changed out of all recognition after the war of 1914–1918. Skirts shot up and waists down, bosoms and curves were ruthlessly flattened and the boyish look became all the rage. Hair was shingled ... cut short like a boy's, and worn with little cloche hats which were extremely unbecoming. Only the very slim and young looked good like this. The older generations stuck firmly to long skirts and gowns, sometimes down to the ground like Queen Mary, but the young all tried to look as different as they could.

Dieting, unheard of before (food and health were never mentioned) – also became the rage. Lipstick, and flesh coloured silk stockings often with horrid cotton tops, long necklaces and long cigarette holders became 'de rigueur.' Nearly all the young smoked or pretended to. Shoes were fairly ugly too with instep straps, and heels like lavatory pedestals. I viewed them all with infantile fascination.

My mother fortunately was forty seven by that time so never went to extremes, and gradually by 1930, clothes began to be very pretty again, flattering and elegant with slender waists and long slim skirts. Evening dresses of chiffon floated and trailed romantically, and hair, much longer was smoothed close to the head and shone like treacle. My parents, like most Naval Officer's families, could not afford to be very fashionable but I loved seeing their smart friends, especially at lunch or dinner parties. We children only saw the dinner party guests through the bannisters in our nightgowns, but at lunch we sat at a separate table with our governess and I could take stock of the fashions to my heart's content!

The younger women and girls were beautifully made up with bright lipstick and mascara, immaculate matt complexions and long red nails. Looking well groomed was essential. Too much make-up was considered theatrical and very bad form, and so were garish exaggerated clothes. Women wanted to be admired, not stared at. My mother used no make up at all except powder, which was a pity because she was always too pale, often due to ill-health. She was still very pretty with a fine Irish skin, but she rather disdained the fashionable, seldom used creams or lotions either and never scent. This may have been to please my father who, like many men hated make-up on their wives but greatly admired the beautiful ladies who came to the house, all of whom used it!

Red nails drove many older men beserk. They loathed it. 'You look as if you had been gutting rabbits!' they would rage. The girls took no notice at all. Much later when I was fifteen and experimenting with make-up I remember being terribly cowed by an old Admiral who saw the results and commanded me to 'Go upstairs AT ONCE and SCRAPE your face!' He clearly thought make-up was the sign of a Bad Woman! At that age I knew nothing at all about bad women, or 'tarts' as they were called, and needless to say had never seen one! It was all very bewildering. My own feeling about make-up has always been if it makes you look prettier – use it. Seeing drab, putty coloured faces has always depressed me.

All beauty preparations were then kept right out of sight and shrouded in mystery. A lady's dressing table in the 1920s and '30s bore silverbacked hair brushes, a silver hand mirror and two other silver brushes, a larger one for brushing clothes and a smaller one for brushing hats; also a silver shoe-horn and button-hook for buttoning shoes, or boots though these were already out of fashion. Cut glass bottles and a powder box flanked the looking-glass on either side, and there were silver or brass candlesticks as well and frequently flowers. It looked lovely. My mother did not have a complete silver dressing set, I expect it was too expensive, but she had polished tortoiseshell brushes and a beautifully carved hand glass which my father had made for her.

The men in my life – father, uncles and cousins, all wore tweed knickerbockers with matching jackets in the country, with tweed caps or hats, and very handsome they looked; practical too for wearing with boots in wet weather. Long trousers would have got covered in mud and torn by brambles walking through fields and woods. My father was considered very dashing when he appeared at Oldtown in plus-fours. These were at first just longer, baggier knickerbockers, but they rapidly became the fashion because the Prince of Wales loved them. Later still they became so long and so baggy they looked ridiculous. Grey flannel 'Oxford bags' were worn by some young men, mostly undergraduates, but frightfully frowned on by their elders who thought they looked untidy and sloppy – which they did.

Not till much later did corduroy become the most practical country wear. Then it was looked on as farm labourer's cloth and always had a strong and most peculiar smell when new. On Sundays for church men wore dark blue suits and bowler hats, now seldom seen, or grey flannel suits in summer, and for weddings and funerals always morning-suits with cut away coats which were most elegant. Many of these suits descended through fathers and grandfathers for generations and there was always keen rivalry to see whose was the oldest; the tailor's name and date were to be found inside the breast-pocket. At night of course everyone dressed up.

I had even stronger views about our own clothes. We children had to wear practical ones which stood up to hard wear in the country and schoolroom. Practical, alas, seldom meant pretty. Over this my mother's idea's and mine frequently clashed! I hated 'pull-ups' which were baggy and soft corduroy trousers with long tightly buttoned legs ... rather like shapeless jodhpurs. But they were warm so we had to wear them out of doors, topped by tweed overcoats with velvet collars. In winter we wore corduroy bonnets with rosettes over each ear.

Next our skins we children all wore 'chilpruf' combinations ... strange vest-like garments with legs, made of the very finest wool jersey which started off white but turned deep yellow with age and washing. When older, little girls wore liberty-bodices, long cotton vests with strips of strong tape running down them, which buttoned firmly up the front and disguised anything as indiscreet as a budding bosom.

Our Summer frocks were much more popular; flowered cotton with knickers to match. The skirts always covered the knees and children then seldom suffered from acidosis or chills. The dresses were always in pretty pastel colours which showed up pink cheeks and flower-like complexions becomingly. For church we wore straw hats with daisies round them.

Unfortunately to protect these clothes at home my mother made us wear cotton pinafores which we hated, especially as we had to make them ourselves in sewing lessons with our governess. Both Aunt Jane and my mother sewed quite beautifully with almost invisible stitches, but our efforts never came anywhere near theirs and were viewed with disgust. Socks and stockings went into holes at once in those pre-nylon days, so hours were also spent darning, over wooden mushrooms, even more unpopular, when we longed to be out in the woods and garden playing games.

Children's parties and dancing classes were special occasions when we wore silk taffeta dresses and socks, and bronze pumps with rosettes on them. We learnt Greek and ballroom dancing, and Scottish reels, also to curtsey gracefully, necessary for when presented at Court or to important people. Very pretty this looked with one's skirts billowing round one like a flower. Little boys came to dancing class too and usually loathed it. Twenty five years later I was much amused when taking my small nieces and nephew to their dancing class to find things there had scarcely changed. When the mistress said 'Now then! All march round the room in line like brave soldiers, heads up, shoulders back!' alas two of the brave soldiers ... boys ...

were sobbing their hearts out! In our day little boys were made of sterner stuff and more likely to pull our hair or mob things up until their nannies grabbed them. Now, twenty five years later still I suppose all this is history.

My preoccupation with clothes stemmed, I am sure, from lack of self-confidence. I was a plain child, or thought I was, and pretty clothes did wonders for me. I think too it was the beginning of my love of beauty ... of every kind, which has been such a factor in my life, and perhaps helped me to become a successful painter. My sister, a year younger, was very pretty and never seemed to suffer any doubts about clothes. On arriving at one children's party ... all strangers ... with my aunt, Coralie aged four viewed the assembled company and remarked happily in a loud stage-whisper 'We're much the nicest, aren't we!' Aunt Jane, somewhat taken aback but vastly amused replied 'Hush darling, of course you are, but you must NEVER say so!' How I envied such confidence.

Little girls were also taught to please, (I am not so sure about little boys!) Smiles and good manners were the order of the day and my mother patiently explained the value of charm. The nannies, not strong on charm themselves but keen on good behaviour strove hard to instil it. 'You must smile nicely and look interested, especially when you are introduced, and especially to older people,' they would say. I loved meeting people from my earliest years, and rather enjoyed being sent down to the drawingroom to say 'How do you do?' Coralie was less keen. There was one occasion when aged three and four, we arrived all dressed up at the door with nanny and Coralie came to a halt with a fearful scowl. 'If you make me go in there I'll bawl!' she announced furiously, (perhaps her dress was scratching her). 'You'll not bawl!' said Nanny Doyle. 'If you bawl I'll shoot the boots off you!' and pushed her into the room.

Another time my mother came to fetch us from the nursery and whispered 'You must be specially nice to the Blacketts ... they are great friends, and they have come a long way to see you!' I was frightfully impressed and skipped across the drawingroom to Ralph Blackett's knee (making a beeline for the man needless to say), 'Have you come a very long way to see me?' I enquired doubtfully. He was completely bowled over; they had indeed come a long way though not of course to see me! But he became a friend for life.

Punctuality was another virtue everyone sought to instil. In this I was frequently at fault, over the problem of clothes. I could never decide which of two pairs of ugly shoes looked least bad, and so forth. This was not vanity so much as a vast inferiority complex about looking acceptable. I did not expect admiration but I did want the other children to like me. My mother seemed to understand this, especially as my sister looked pretty whatever she wore. My father did not understand, and loathed unpunctuality especially for church. As a result he would be fuming in the car while I still blithered about my socks or whatever, and we would all arrive at church in anything but a Christian frame of mind. He always read the lessons which he did beautifully, but it took me about half an hour to recover.

Strange to say my great-niece Rosie aged five seems to have inherited my problems. Although extremely pretty she too finds it impossible to decide what to wear and is often surrounded by socks while everyone else is yelling from the hall-door. It is worse for her because she has so many more socks. Parents, alas, can never see the difference. I think what partially cured me was firstly despair, and secondly reading in some film magazine ... strictly forbidden ... that the cure for self-consciousness was to walk into a crowded restaurant and wave wildly at some imaginary person on the other side of the room. 'You will find hardly anyone will notice you,' said the magazine. At twelve years old I had never been into a restaurant at all, but I always remembered and found it excellent advice.

The paying and returning of calls by grown-ups was still very much the social custom in 1930. Cocktail parties were not yet the fashion much less invitations to drinks, so it was a good way for people to meet new arrivals and take stock of each other without the rigours of a lunch or dinner party. If one liked them invitations followed; if not, the formalities had been observed. It was really a very civilised custom which had been going strong for over a hundred years, but was only possible if one had leisure and domestic staff.

I loved going with my mother in the car when, nicely dressed, she was paying calls. She often took me with her if it was not too far away and would point out interesting things as we drove along, birds, flowers or buildings. There was almost no traffic in the country then and cars only went at twenty five or thirty miles an hour so this was not as hazardous as it sounds! I was filled with curiosity about everything new; there was always the chance that the people we were calling on would have a child of my age, or at least an animal of sorts. Often there would be a lovely house up a long drive with ancient trees.

'Calling' was usually done by married ladies and followed a distinct pattern. Newcomers to the county, or community, if it was the Navy or Army, were called upon first by ladies of similar rank and age who had heard about them on the social grapevine. They arrived about 3.15.pm taking cards in a little monogrammed silver case. The door would be opened by a parlourmaid or footman who was asked if Mrs So and So was 'at home?' The maid would then bear the visitor's card off on a silver salver to her mistress, who upon seeing who it was, would tell the maid she was indeed 'at home', and the caller was duly led to the drawingroom and announced. A first call would only last about fifteen minutes, exchanging pleasantries, and then the visitor would take herself off unless pressed to stay to tea. Upon departing she would leave on the salver with the maid two of her own cards and one of her husband's for the other husband; husbands did not leave cards on the unknown wife. If there was a grown-up daughter a card was left for her as well. In some houses, including my great-aunt Mabel's, Black Hall in Kildare, there was a large stuffed brown bear standing upright by the hall door, and it held the salver for departing cards. Altogether one got through quite a lot of cards!

Within a week the call had to be returned and this would follow the same pattern. When we did this I would be left in the car on my best behaviour, and mama would say after a suitable interval, 'well I must be on my way, I have left my little daughter in the car.' Whereupon the hostess might say 'Oh, wouldn't you like to bring her in?' Then I would be inspected and either sent off to join the resident young or given a picture book to look at while the grown-ups talked.

If one called and the owner was not 'at home' one simply left the cards with the maid, or the bear, turning up one corner to show one had called in person, and duty was done.

Sending cards with a coachman or the chauffeur was rude. 'Not at home' could mean just that, or else that the lady of the house had a splitting headache or something. In this case she should have warned the maid in advance that she would not be 'at home' to callers. It was considered very bad form if one's card was taken in and she then said she was 'not at home'. There were of course endless nuances. Not to be called on was a frightful setback, and delay in calling rather rude. Very young brides often dreaded it and suffered agonies of shyness when an autocratic matron descended on them; Bee Sackville of Drayton who had married at eighteen told me she used to run up onto the roof and peer through the balustrade until she saw the car drive away.

The last call I can remember my mother paying was shortly before the last war. She called on the young wife of a new bishop, and was distinctly shocked to find the baby sitting on its pot in the middle of the drawing-room floor with toys and nappies strewn around and the mother looking distraught amidst it all. Needless to say the visit was not a success from any point of view!

After the war this way of life vanished. So many things go overboard in war, the good and the bad, and many of them never return.

CHAPTER 6

BATHS AND THINGS

BY FAR THE NICEST BATH I ever had was in Dorset. It was a hip bath set upon towels in front of a glowing kitchen range, the black iron sort with twinkling brass handles on the oven doors. Being only four years old the warm water covered me almost to my neck, the firelight flickered on the whitewashed walls, and I positively beamed with bliss. The year must have been 1927, and I was staying with my nursery governess, Miss Foot, at her parents' farm so that both my parents, who had been ill, could have a badly needed holiday alone. 'Footie's' mother hovered round with more warm towels to rub me dry afterwards. We were living in Dorset then because my father was commanding HMS Vulcan, the submarine flotilla depot ship in Portland harbour. 'Footie' was teaching me to read and write. I loved her, and she inexplicably seems to have been very fond of me. It must have been June because I remember we took big baskets of lunch out to her father and brothers in the fields, and some of them were wearing smocks over their corduroy trousers. I was wearing a smock too, and a pink sun bonnet! The sun was shining, larks were singing, and the air was full of the smell of new-mown hay. We all sat happily munching home-made bread, cheese and ham under a hedge, the men no doubt drinking home-made beer or cider too.

This glimpse of farm life in those long gone days has remained with me; partly because I have only once stayed on a real English farm since, and partly I suspect because baths in the big old country houses that were my parents' homes in Ireland were nothing like such bliss. Bathrooms then were in a transitional stage. Before that grown-ups also had hip-baths in front of their bedroom fire, though inevitably less submerged; but now real bathrooms were being discreetly installed in rooms far away down a long cold passage.

Often there were two baths together with a wooden partition between which, for some reason, did not go right to the ceiling, so that one could lie and chat to the invisible occupant of the neighbouring bath. This arrangement was at first mostly for men and children, married ladies did not want to be seen in bath caps and curling pins without any make-up, so

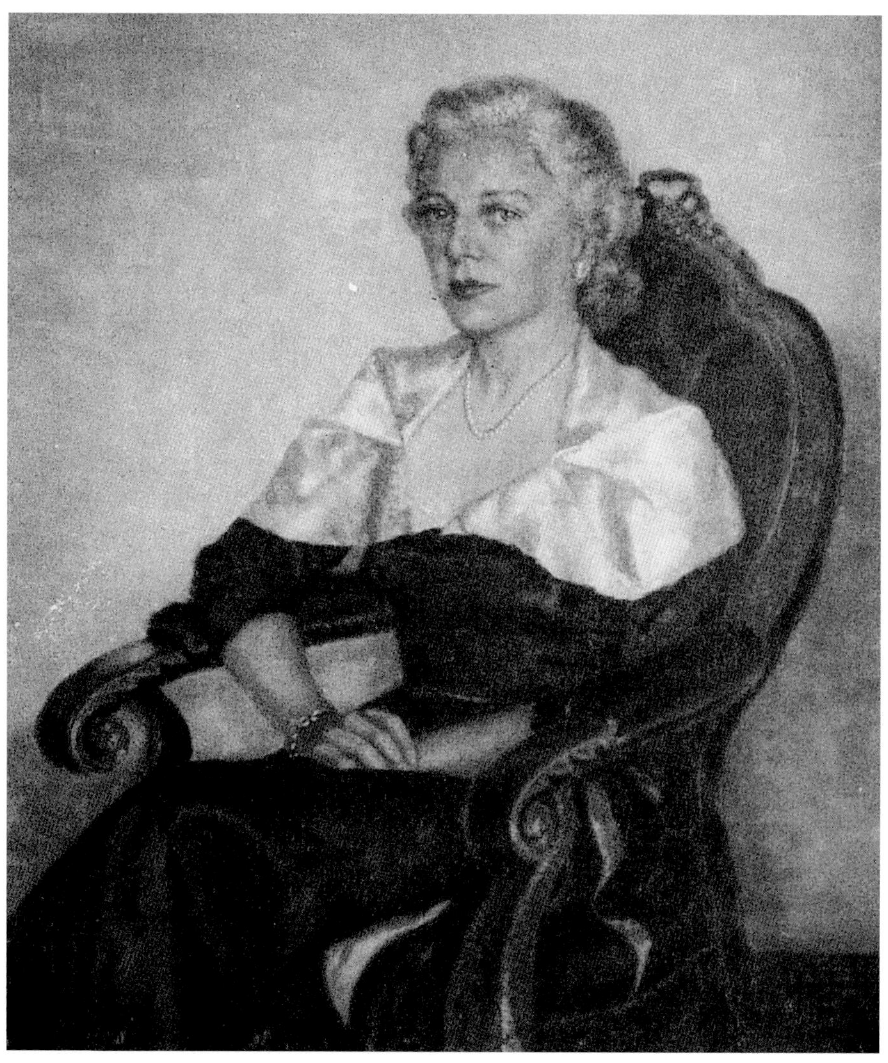

My painting of Nita, Mrs Madden of Hilton Park, 1950

continued to enjoy hipbaths in their rooms. No children were allowed to loll in baths. At Oldtown, my father's home, when we stayed there for Christmas, there was always a queue of nannies with more children waiting their turn to take over.

Years and years later in 1948 many of the same bathrooms were still going strong far away down the same cold passages. The one at Parkanaur near Dungannon was so cold that if the water was more than tepid the steam was so thick one could hardly find the bath. At Hilton, in County

Monaghan, it was much more snug tucked away in the nursery wing. Here, being now grown-up we could wallow at length and exchange confidences and advice with the unseen occupant beyond the partition in the neighbouring bath. The Madden children, then very small boys, loved running my bath and stuck transfers of butterflies upon the sides. They were darlings, adored the smell of bath salts, and would happily have stayed with me throughout.

The problem in big old houses was of course the plumbing. There was none. The walls were very thick, so even lavatories were few and far between; except at Balcaskie where my Anstruther cousins lived. There some more recent antecedent had installed sixteen lavatories ... it was a very big house! ... mostly in the towers, but still just two far away bathrooms. It is a beautiful early 17th century house, the two main floors being show pieces of William Bruce architecture and plasterwork. Relations however, and even Madge herself, Mrs Anstruther, always slept up on the fourth ... the nursery ... floor even when I was grown-up.

Castle Coole in Co. Fermanagh is a superb Wyatt house and no doubt equally hard to plumb. The Belmores who had only recently inherited it then lived snugly in one of the wings. Visitors slept in the main block which had vast spare bedrooms. I loved staying there not only because Gaby Belmore was one of the most charming delightful men I have ever met, but because I always slept like a top in an old four-poster bed with a thick, soft feather mattress. In summer, when the high windows were open, swallows flew in and out in the sunlight. The bath one used there was in a former dressing-room across the upstairs hall. It stood in splendid isolation on four paw feet in the middle of the linoleum floor, and the water was velvety soft off the peat. When my cousin David stayed at another stately home for a dance he advanced on a similar bathroom and found Lord H – who was English, basking happily in dark deep brown water. 'Come in!' he said, 'It's alright, it's the water, not me!' Nowadays a peat bath like that cost a fortune in health clinics.

The worst bath I ever had was also in Fermanagh. My hostess had spent some years in Japan. Now married and living in Ireland she had installed there a Japanese bath set up, and was quite determined I should reap its benefits. She stood over me to see I did it right. The room was an icy cold marble terrazzo box. I stripped down and made a beeline for the bath which I had filled with hot water, only to be hauled back by N ... who conducted me to a horrible little tap in the wall with a piece of soap and a bowl beside it. It seemed one had to wash oneself clean all over at the tap ... cold of course ... before daring to get in and pollute the bathwater. I couldn't help wondering whether her husband was forced to have Japanese baths too, but when I stayed with them later in a very hot country thank goodness the baths were all the good old comforting British sort.

Clonhugh in Westmeath also had swallows flitting into the spare bedrooms in summer and huge feather beds for dreamless sleep; and Lough Bawn near Castleblayney had bats that squeaked in the billiard room cupboard, which I loved. In those days people in Ireland ... and Scotland ... lived close to nature and enjoyed it. We also rather enjoyed the hysterics of others used to more sheltered lives who screamed at the sight of a mouse or bat. One great friend of mine did let out a scream when interviewing her cook in the basement kitchen. The cook had politely lifted a cushion off one of the kitchen armchairs for her to take a seat and three mice jumped out.

She leapt onto the table and was severely admonished by her husband, who happened to be passing at that moment on his way to the gun-room, for screaming in front of the servants. 'Sure t'was just the unexpectedness av it,' said the cook comfortingly.

Nature was less popular when a fox got into the hen run and killed all the hens. But by and large it compensated for the cold, damp and other difficulties, and where else but Ireland could one hear then the call of a corncrake, wrens singing their hearts out in the mornings, a fox barking at night ... or swallows flying round one's bed. Of course it was often uncomfortable but people were used to this. Even in Nothumberland Sir Hugh B ... was once staying for a shoot at a neighbouring house in the '30s without his wife.

The spare room had twin beds, then very newfangled, and later, next day, the hostess was somewhat taken aback when her young housemaid gasped 'Oh madam! The gentleman slept in the wrong bed, the one I had not made-up, and I had left the fire-irons in it!'

Now much is changed. Gone is the dear, eccentric domestic staff who made such houses possible. En suite bathrooms and even bidets are quite common, the food may be nouvelle cuisine and the guests may be paying; but gone too is the corncrake.

CHAPTER 7

CONWAY AND NORTHERN IRELAND

AFTER THE DEATH OF my last grandparent in 1931 I did not return to Ireland until I was nineteen in the middle of the war. My father, who had retired from the Royal Navy also in 1931 had studied estate management at the Lee in Lanarkshire, which belonged for her life to his aunt Lady de Robeck through her first husband Sir Simon Lockhart. During this time we lived happily in Dumfriesshire and he soon became Land Agent to several small estates in the North. Then in 1935 he took over the management of the great Dean and Chapter of Durham and Lord Crewe Trust estates ranging from Berwick on Tweed to the Tees.

It was for this reason that we moved to Co. Durham and bought Witton Hall where we lived for most of the next seventeen years.

My father was recalled to the Navy before the outbreak of war in 1939; Naval Officers are always on the Reserve, and he served with distinction for the duration, including both the Norway campaign and the Landings in Normandy. Of these years I have written at length in 'Lydia's Story', their joys and sorrows, hopes and fears. I joined the Women's Royal Naval Service as soon as I was eighteen and worked at Bletchley Park in the now famous Ultra Enigma code-breaking section as a very junior Wren. It was on sick-leave from the Wrens that I came again to Ulster, to recuperate with my aunt at Conway, near Dunmurry.

At that time there was a large number of troops stationed in Northern Ireland, many of them American, training for the invasions of North Africa and Normandy, as well as the British troops for the defence of the country. The South of Ireland had remained neutral, but as that had never stopped Hitler invading any of the other countries he now occupied there was always a possible danger. Occupation of the South by Germany would have cut off vital supplies from America to the Allies and there was also the problem of German spying installations, and submarines refuelling there from remote beaches.

In Ulster the great shipping, linen, textile and other industries were working to capacity and there was employment for everyone, including many who came up from the South to work in them. Farming was also booming and there was nothing like the shortage of food that civilians in Great Britain experienced. Everyone who could kept chickens, ducks and pigs, even in the backyards of Belfast terraced houses. A flourishing smuggling trade went on in both directions across the border, and despite the officials on both sides striving to prevent it, great was the ingenuity of the smugglers, of all walks of life! Meat, on the hoof no doubt, butter, cheese, drink and silk stockings flowed up North – until they ran out; while tea, coffee, sugar and coal flowed down. On the Dublin to Belfast train every guile was employed in the smuggling from hiding things in ventilators to hanging goods out of the carriage windows on the off side to the platform when the customs men came round. This worked like a dream until they got wise to it. There was very little petrol or oil in the South, and I remember the vast bastions of turf that lined all the roads in the Phoenix Park, stored there to keep the Dublin homefires burning. Nor was it unknown for country trains there to grind to a halt for lack of fuel, and for the passengers to descend and collect firewood or even fencing posts so that they could stoke the boiler and proceed.

Although there was no conscription in Northern Ireland nearly all my friends' and relations' sons, husbands or daughters were away in the armed forces; but apart from this the life there was little changed from my childhood days. There was still plenty of domestic staff ... mostly people too old or too young for war work, and social life still seemed to flourish. Many women ran canteens, the Red Cross, and did other voluntary work. One of the biggest canteens was at the Pollock Dock, Belfast, for all seamen and dockyard workers. It was manned till late at night and must have been a haven of warmth and good food for all sailors after the horrors of war at sea. Not all the horrors were at sea. One night four of the poor ladies driving home from work on the night shift at the canteen in the total blackout ... all car lights were hooded and reduced to slits, mistook the way, drove into the dock and Mrs. McCammon, Mrs Harrison, Miss Glass and Mrs Jefferson were all drowned.

It seems strange now to think that within a radius of twenty five miles of Conway no less than twenty six of our friends and relations then had titles, either bestowed on them for public works and achievements or inherited, and most of them lived in large and beautiful houses; others were country landowners, and nearly all were either in the Government at Stormont or Westminster, managing their own flourishing businesses, farming, or engaged in public and charitable duties both physically and financially. As almost none of these families ... or their houses ... once so prominent in Ulster remain today it may be of interest to mention some of them for the record.

At that time my mother's sister, Aunt Jane Campbell, was hostess to Sir John Milne Barbour at Conway, then still his family home. His wife, an

American cousin, had died tragically young. When his youngest daughter Betzé wanted to get married and their old governess who was holding the fort had died she begged my aunt, who had very little money of her own, to take over as hostess at Conway. War was imminent in 1938 and Aunt Jane, who suffered from bronchitis and incipient pneumonia, knew she would no longer be able to spend the winters abroad, which in those days was much cheaper and warmer. She was therefore delighted to take on this

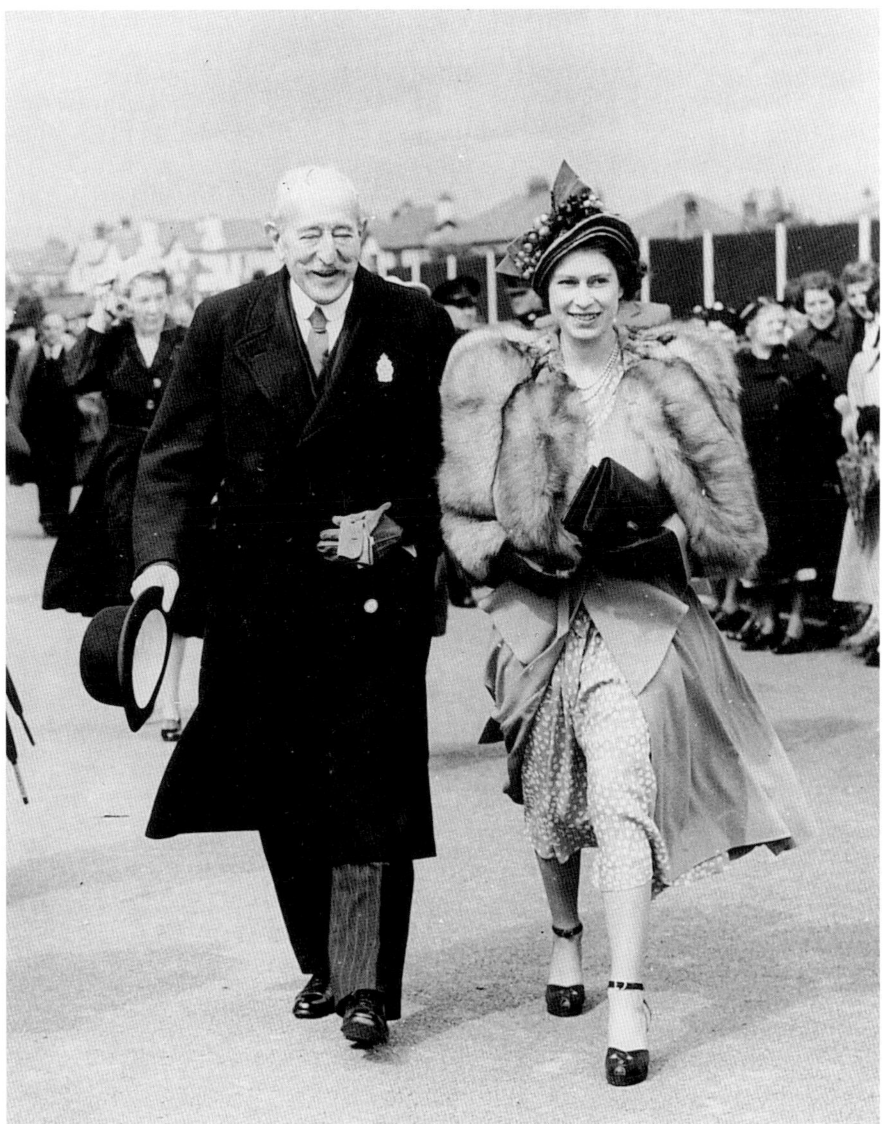

Sir J. Milne Barbour with Princess Elizabeth at Balmoral Show, 1949

job. Sir Milne was Minister of Finance in the Ulster Government and also the owner and Chairman of the Linen Thread Company which had worldwide connections, with mills at Hilden, Lisburn and elsewhere, to which he still walked the few miles along the Lagan every day after breakfast. He had a chauffeur and several cars but he believed in keeping fit and saving petrol, and greatly loved the scenery and country of which he was so proud. Although a considerable potentate he was a quite delightful, courtly old man who looked so like Adolph Menjou, then a well-known film actor, that in America he was often mistaken for him

It was here to Conway that I came on sick-leave in 1943, worn and ill though barely grown-up. No-one could have been kinder than Auntie and Sir Milne; and no-one could have been better fitted to act as his hostess than she. She was a marvellous organiser, an expert manager of staff, and loved entertaining. She also knew everyone. Sir Milne loved parties and people and they both loved bridge. He was a very rich man but had suffered not only the loss of his young wife but also of his only son who had been killed in a flying accident some years before. Although Elsa Maxwell had been doing the much the same sort of job as hostess, freelance, in the United States for some years, it was considered quite an innovation in Ulster, despite the age of both Sir Milne and my Aunt! He was quite unaware of this and my aunt simply rose above the gossip. His married daughter Mary Byers lived at Longhurst nearby and was devoted to them both.

How lucky I was. Conway was then a perfect capsule of Victorian-Edwardian taste, with American overtones like marvellous central heating. It was extremely comfortable, quite unlike most of the big country houses I knew so well, including my grandfather's, which were much older and had

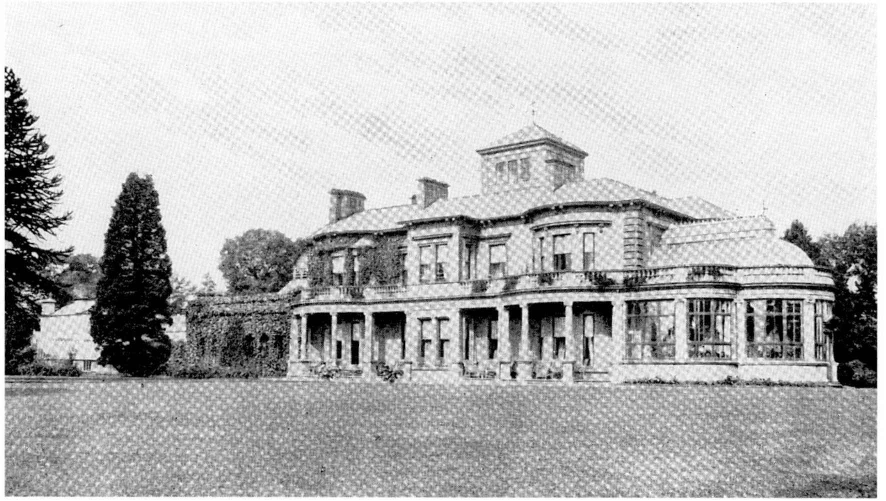

Conway, Dunmurry. The Garden Front, 1947

lovely Georgian furniture and paintings, but were generally cold, rather shabby, and with the inevitable lack of bathrooms. At Conway these were all 'en suite.' The great drawingroom ran the width of the house and the walls were covered with rose silk damask. The curtains were red velvet swagged with heavy gold braid, and more curtains could divide the room into two. There were large gilded looking- glasses on the walls, Victorian portraits, comfortable ottomans and sofas, and masses of beautiful potted plants ... azaleas, palms, gloxinias, cinnerarias and rhododendrons in which my aunt took great pride. Leading out of this there was a large conservatory full of more lovely plants. The hall and stairway were panelled in dark mahogany, and there were suits of armour, weapons and ornaments ... but no bear! Sir Milne did not shoot; but there was a large tiger skin on the floor, complete with head, over which we young all regularly tripped coming home at night in the blackout, knocking out its teeth. There was also a very large lobster made of bronze and beautifully jointed which lived in the grate of the never-used fireplace and fascinated me. On the polished floors were Persian rugs which slithered about, and fine 'Turkish' carpets made in Donegal.

Outside there was a cricket ground, putting-green, lovely gardens, and a big swimming pool beside the tennis courts which had their own Greek pavilion for changing in and for having tea. There was a home – farm and stabling for many horses and cars (in which a General and his staff lived during the war) and along the avenue were several enormous totem poles presented to Sir Milne in N. America many years before. Alas, where are all these things now? Almost nothing remains and Conway, rebuilt, is now an hotel.

Sir Milne's sister, Nellie Harland, lived nearby at Dunmurry and he was devoted to her, as was my aunt. She often came to play Bridge and was a charming little old lady whose first husband had been Thomas Andrews, Managing Director of Harland and Wolff, where the 'Titanic' of tragic memory was built. He deliberately went down with the ship when she struck an iceberg and sank in 1912, with enormous loss of life. The 'Titanic' had been considered unsinkable, so not only were there not enough lifeboats, but many passengers refused to leave the ship until it was too late because they could not believe she was doomed. She had, in my humble opinion, been going far too fast in ice-infested waters in order to break some record on this, her maiden voyage. But this was not Thomas Andrew's fault. An exceedingly brave man, his life had been especially hard because he was the nephew of Lord Pirrie, Chairman of Harland and Wolff, who expected him to work harder and longer starting at the bottom, than any dockyard worker. He joined the company aged sixteen, starting work at 6 a.m. and was treated with undue harshness by his childless uncle even for those strict Victorian days; and he was only on board 'Titanic' because

Lord Pirrie who should have sailed in her was ill and in hospital. Nellie must have been a very attractive girl because both Andrews and Henry Harland wanted to marry her. Sometime after his death she did marry Henry Harland, who was also very good-looking, and in spite of such tragedy always seemed a sweet and happy person with her three daughters.

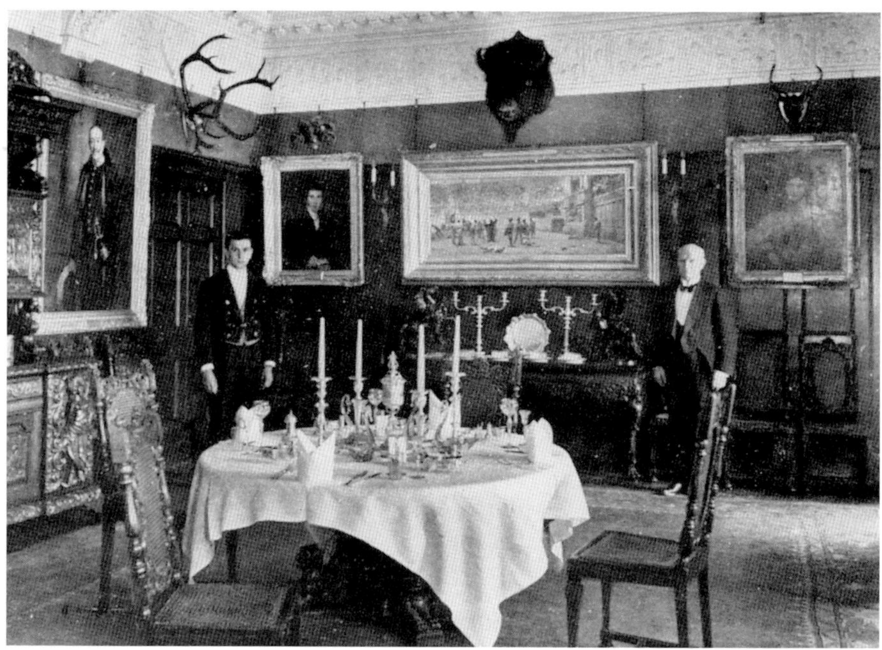

Conway, the dining room with Footman Albert and Dugan the Butler, 1947

A strange footnote to the 'Titanic' disaster is that my mother had an dreadful premonition that it was going to sink, being so widely hailed as unsinkable. Herself married to a Submariner she and my father were only too aware of the strength of the sea and the frailty of ships, and felt it was tempting Providence to claim that anything was unsinkable.

Another close neighbour to Conway at Seymour Hill, then a fine country house with large grounds, was Colonel Arthur Charley and his wife who were elderly and delightful, and also came to play bridge. They had no children, and alas he was later killed during the felling of trees at Seymour Hill. His nephew Robin is a distinguished historian of the Ulster Regiments in which he served; but Seymour Hill is now a sprawling housing estate, and the little Ballybog lane up which I used to ride aged nineteen is no longer recognisable.

In 1943 the General living in the stables and his A.D.C. ate with us, and despite the shortages of petrol and much else social life still flourished. Sir

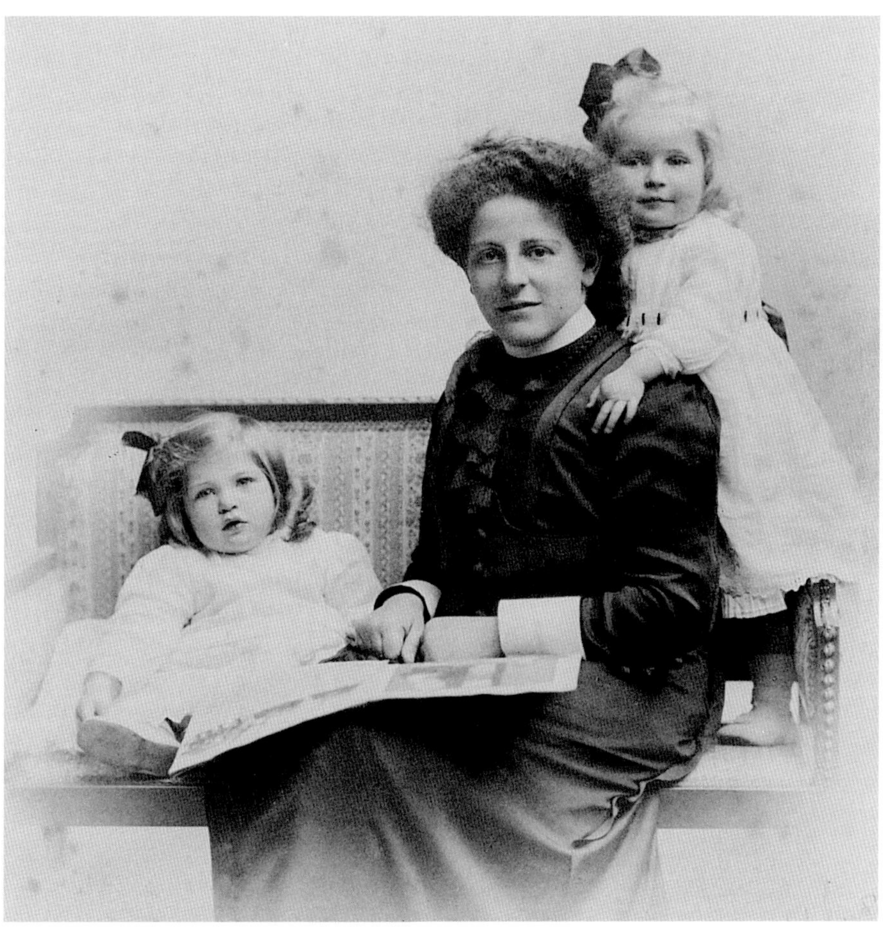

Nellie, widow of Thomas Andrews with left, daughter 'Elba' and right, neice Betzé Barbour. (By kind permission of Mrs Elise Coburn).

Milne had bought my aunt an old Ormeau Bakery van which ran on batteries for a radius of twenty to thirty miles; the batteries were charged up at night. There was then still a wide railway network, Sir Milne was a Director of the Great Northern Railway, and the Derriaghy Halt was at the bottom of the avenue so many of their friends arrived by train.

Amongst these was Lord Enniskillen from Florencecourt and his second wife, both excellent bridge-players. I once walked down to the station with him when he was returning to Fermanagh and wanted to catch the Dublin train and change at Portadown. 'Oh,' I said, 'I thought it did not stop at Derriaghy?' 'No,' he replied modestly, 'But it said it would stop for me!' Trains were very obliging in those long gone days, and he turned out to be a director too of course. He was said to have a fiery temper and that was why his first wife left him, but we always got on famously, perhaps because I was never afraid of him. He sometimes said he wished I would marry his son Michael who was in the Irish Guards ... this was after the war ... but Michael I knew was already enamoured of a dashing but much older widow; of them more anon.

Other frequent visitors to Conway were Sir George and Lady Clark of Seapark; he was Chairman of the Great Northern Railway; Sir Basil Brooke the Prime Minister (known widely as 'Sir Bawzil') a charming and amusing man ... later Lord Brookborough, and his wife, (bossy, but also amusing ... he adored her); the Cecil Lindsays of Lissue House, and Sir Christopher and Lady Musgrave of Norwood Tower at Strandtown, whose son Dick became a great friend of my sister's and mine when he returned from the war.

It was all so informal and relaxed, or so it seemed. These delightful elderly people, fifty years older than I was, still worked hard as administrators, though many like the Brookes and Musgraves had already lost beloved sons killed in the war. Their courage, good temper and kindness never faltered, and when able, they loved an evening in the

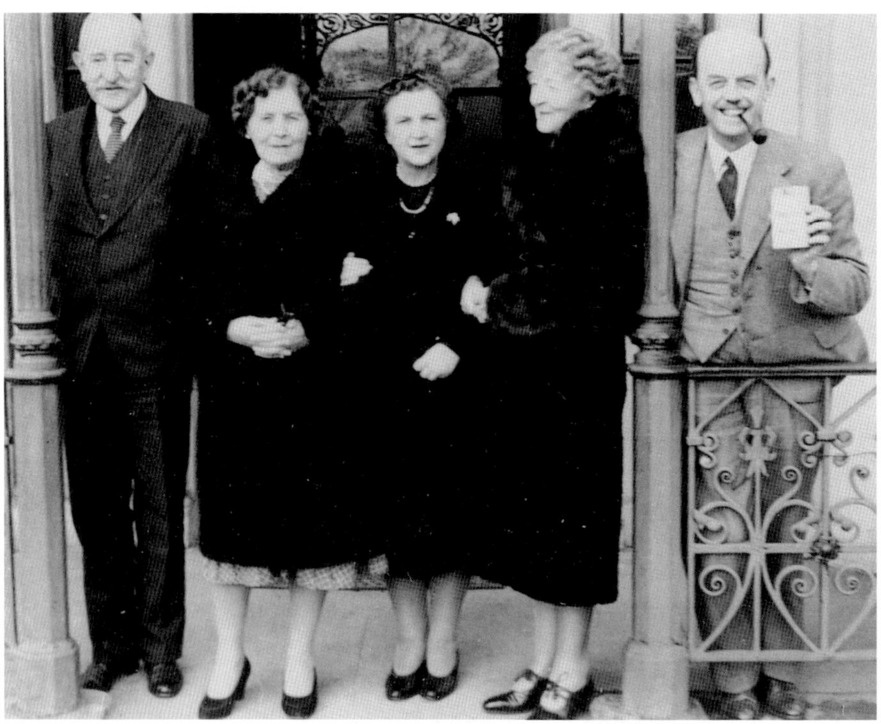

Sir Milne, Aunt Jane, Lady Musgrave, Mrs Armitage-Moore and Sir Christopher Musgrave

company of old friends. The conversation was witty and erudite, the food ... all home grown ... delicious, and the bridge afterwards took their minds for a time off the war, of the end of which there was still little sign. The staff who waited on us consisted of Dugan the butler who was over eighty and Albert the footman who was eighteen and later went on to become butler at Government House, where he reigned for many years together with Rugman who had been my aunt's personal maid, and with whom we kept in touch for many years too.

Other friends who came to Conway were the Armitage-Moores from Rowallane, famous for its gardens which they had created. Mrs Armitage-Moore wore a fringe, rather like Queen Alexandra, and amazed me once by saying she had never been into a butcher's shop in her life ... I suppose her cook telephoned the orders ... she was then well over eighty. All those who came by train of course stayed the night.

Occasionally, to forget the war with its burdens and sorrows, these distinguished older men let off steam, and once I was lucky enough to be there, staying with the Hermans at Necarne Castle in Co. Fermanagh when Dick Herman gave a rat shooting dinner party. He was not actually living in the Castle. The army was occupying it and the Hermans were squashed into the herds's house nearby.

Dick, being over age or under strength for the army, was rearing 400 pigs in the stable yards and sheds round about to produce much needed food for the war effort. Unfortunately the pigs needed food too so he had to store a lot of grain and meal, and in those wartime days there was a great swill-collecting organisation as well. Inevitably this brought huge numbers of rats who revelled in the bonanza.

There may be some people who like rats ... I have yet to meet them ... in which case they had better skip what follows.

We loathed them; they not only ate much of the pigs food but contaminated the rest with their droppings, and rat urine is highly poisonous, spreading disease amongst humans as well. So whenever his friends could get away he and his wife 'Cosy' (Coralie) invited them to a rat shoot. The rats did not appear until after dark so we all had a good dinner in scruff clothes first. The guests on this occasion were the Prime Minister Sir Basil Brooke, Colonel Charley Alexander, and Sir Harry Mulholland, Speaker of the Government at Stormont; all well over fifty.

We sallied forth in macintoshes and gumboots ... there was a fine drizzle ... armed with .22 rifles. I was given a torch and a golf club. Dick knew exactly where the rats would be and everyone was placed strategically round each shed or looking over the door, in silence and the dark. When we switched on the torches there were the rats. Then followed the most brilliant shooting I have ever seen.

Rats were picked off sitting between the legs of bullocks, perched on the troughs while the pigs ate, and running up drainpipes to the rafters. It was amazing; no-one missed, and the cattle did not even move. I suppose they were used to it. All I had to do was follow a rat with my torch for someone. Finally Dick parked me outside the swill shed.

'I'll just go and rattle the barrels' he said , 'and the rats will run out and turn left round the corner past you. Your job is to hit them with the golf club as they turn.'

He did, and it was so. Never much of a hand at golf, I turned out to have a natural talent for golfing rats. Was this a ladylike accomplishment? It was not; but I have seldom enjoyed myself more! Next day everyone was back at work coping with governing, casualty lists, rationing and the blackout.

At that time of the war there was a branch of the army in Northern Ireland known as B.T.N.I., which for a long time I thought was Beatty and I and wondered why we never met Beatty. It stood for British Troops, Northern Ireland. I am not sure what their function was but many of them were retired officers, recalled, from well-known South of Ireland families. Among those who were great fun were the Stafford-King-Harmans of Rockingham whose only son Tom was killed in 1944, and the Ffrenchs of Ffrenchs' Court, now a ruin. Rockingham, a lovely Nash house, was completely gutted by fire in 1957 while the King-Harmans were away, and after standing like a ghostly skeleton for some years was demolished, and the demesne is now a recreation park.

Although I longed for friends of my own age I loved these charming old people who were so kind and complimentary to a very young girl, and being on sick-leave I was still far from well. But I did enjoy their parties ... everyone still wore evening dress even if it was old and mended, and after dinner I sewed while they played bridge. I made used silk parachutes ... they were all pure silk in those pre-nylon days, it was so strong ... into petticoats and nightgowns, for clothing was very strictly rationed. I remember the men being greatly intrigued by this and my aunt being not at all sure it was suitable to be sewing underclothes in public! The parachutes were all long tapered strips cut on the bias, which the men had never heard of before, and which greatly complicated matters necessitating many joins.

Sometimes my aunt took me to tea with Sir Thomas and Lady Dixon at Dixon Park. Lady Dixon was Scottish, slightly formidable and very rich. Sir Thomas was the younger brother of Lord Glentoran, (who had once wanted to marry my aunt Coralie de Burgh). We had tea in the blue and gold drawing room, and in those days tea always consisted of hot scones and honeycomb, wafer thin sandwiches, and several cakes. As we ate very little I imagine most of it was enjoyed later in the servants' hall. The Dixons had no children and left Dixon Park to the City of Belfast when they died; the house became an old people's home, and the grounds are now the famous rose gardens and public park. The number of big houses belonging to people who could afford a big staff was fairly limited even then, and most of them knew each other. After the war there was always a shortage of trained staff, and even at the 'makee-learn' stage these tended to do the rounds, either because they did not like the place, or each other, or because they just wanted a change.

After Albert we had an even younger footman called Percy at Conway. He came to us from S ... where it seemed he was not a great success. 'Percy is a very bad boy!' her Ladyship told my aunt on the telephone. We heard later on the usual grapevine that he had called her an old B ...! so he must have been brave, but I don't think he lasted long at Conway either. Then there was Mrs Clarke, a really excellent cook who ruled the kitchen wisely and well and was in great demand. Having met her first at Conway, I next met her at Parkanaur, and later still at Ballywalter Park where she stayed for many years. She always took a great interest in the visitors and knew I loved good food! So I always got a welcome. A vast amount of news and gossip filtered through to the servants' hall, overheard by those waiting on us at table, also about those who left their bedrooms in a mess, or gave trouble; and quite a lot of this filtered back upstairs to us again too!

Girls of my age hated having their clothes unpacked as we were only too aware how old and shabby they were, both during and after the war!

Occasionally there were disasters like one English butler who seemed to have 'mislaid' all the vintage champagne. Sir Milne and my aunt never went near the cellars, they seldom drank even at parties, but having asked for two bottles of champagne to celebrate something it turned out that every bottle had been emptied and filled up with sand. Of course there was no way of telling by whom.

Uncle Toby Campbell was also my godfather and I stayed with him then and after the war at Derrynoose Rectory. He was Rector of Keady and Derrynoose and financial secretary to the Primate. The old rectory, now a ruin, had a lovely garden, and fields where they kept cows for their own milk. He and Aunt Elsie were expert gardeners; their son Morris was in the Army in India, and they had his two tortoises 'Dilly' and 'Dally', known far and wide as the Rectory Crabs because no-one then had seen a tortoise before. Dilly and Dally were great walkers and they were often retrieved far away by interested parishioners who came across them on their travels.

Sometimes I bicycled to the Manor House at which many of my friends' sisters were at school. I do not know how strong it was academically but it produced charming, capable girls, and in those days to be clever was still socially disastrous. Elm Park, the preparatory school for little boys was equally successful and only a few miles away, but when I bicycled there to see cousins they all looked half-starved and I felt awful being given tea as a grown-up young lady by the headmaster in the conservatory while the boys could only watch us eating through the glass.

On the whole though it was a very gracious way of life, devoid of arrogance or showing off, and I was still too young to realize it was already in its twilight. At that time all one could think of was longing for the war to end, and that there was no way of knowing how or if it ever would.

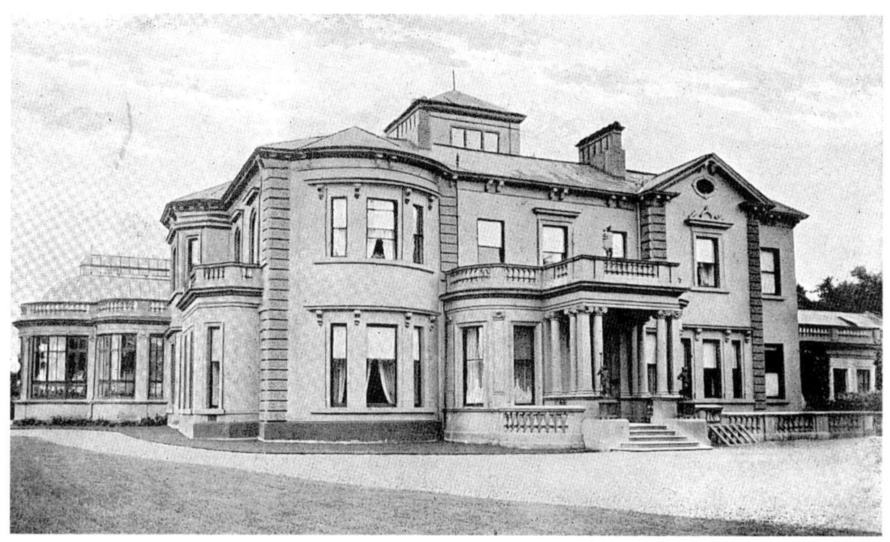

Conway, front entrance, 1939

CHAPTER 8

CONWAY AND NORTHERN IRELAND

PART 2

WHEN THE WAR DID END we were still living at Witton Hall in the North of England and my father, released once more from the Navy, was trying to train a young land agent to take over from him at the Dean and Chapter Office. Both my parents were worn out by six long years of war with all its hardships for my father, and much else of which I have written in 'Lydia's Story'. My mother, who was four years his senior was nearly seventy and almost as tired. Witton was now far too big to manage without help, and Coralie and I had to go and study for careers in London where we would be able to live in the attic of Pierce Synnott, a family friend from Kildare.

I had worked for the Red Cross in Durham after being invalided out of the WRNS so had been living at home and helping there; but our chief joy over the next few years was going over to Ireland for holidays.

Sir Milne and my aunt were still at Conway, and with the ending of petrol rationing I was now able to go much further afield. At Seapark Sir George Clark was dead and Lady Clark was considered something of a dragon, but she had wonderful taste and the house was beautiful, especially the indoor flowers which she arranged to match the colouring in every room. Huge windows opened onto the sea so the house was full of light and sunshine.

Her sons were all good at games; once when I went to play tennis there we were foiled by rain, so went to look at some young bloodstock of theirs instead. I was wearing my best brown and white striped canvas shoes which had belonged to my mother, and walking through the wet grass I suddenly noticed that they were covered in bubbles ... from the cleaning fluid I had used! 'Good Lord' said Tony, 'I've heard of people foaming at the mouth before but never foaming at the feet!' Not long after that Seapark was sold

Tony, now the new Sir George, moved to Co. Down, and the house is now run as an institution. At Florencecourt in Fermanagh Michael Cole had survived the wars, and I loved staying with his parents, the Enniskillens. Sadly he died soon after from a tumour on the brain, quite unsuspected. He had always suffered from epilepsy, and for this reason had not married, but had the aforementioned marvellous girlfriend whom he always called Perkins though this was not her name. A fashionable widow, much older than he, she was devoted to him and lived in London where we all often met. Michael was a dear, not clever, but an excellent farmer and a first class shot. I remember shooting once at Crom Castle which belongs to Lord Erne, then still a schoolboy ... his father had been killed early in the war. We were on one of the islands in the Lough where many trees had been felled, but no-one had cleared the lop and top, so it was very blind; often one could not see where the other guns were. Michael disliked not having a clear field of fire, and after we were all in place but fairly invisible he announced loudly 'I'm HERE! Anyone who shoots me gets a left and right back!' He was fun, and I never heard him say an unkind word about anyone.

Florencecourt now belongs to the National Trust, and the present Earl of Enniskillen, Andrew, lives in Kenya, where the Cole family had pioneered the country at the beginning of the century and a Cole sister had married the great Lord Delamere who did so much to develop it.

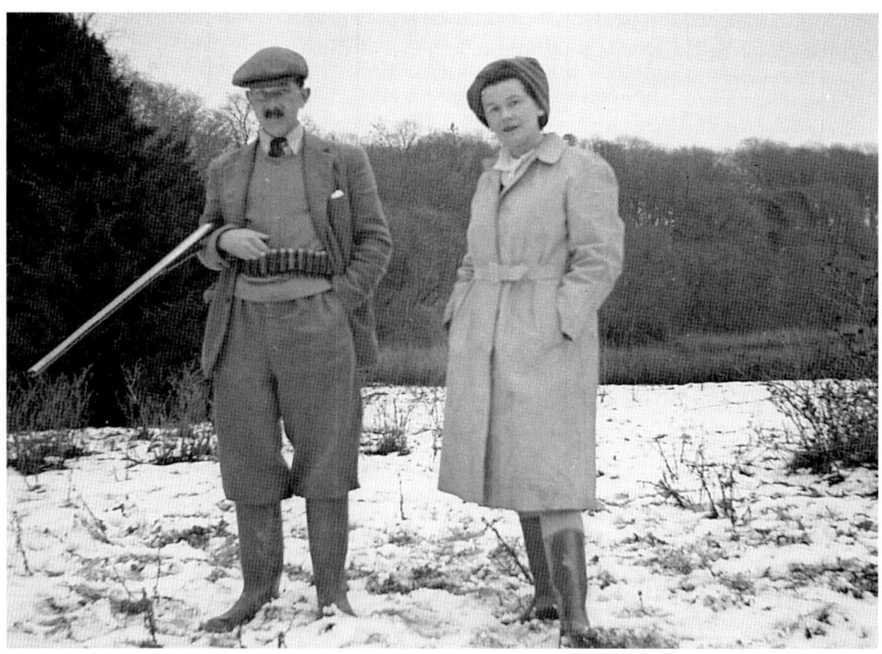

Michael Cole and his sister Frances, 1948

Florencecourt is beautifully kept by the Trust, but without the lively and endearing families who belonged there all such places can be little more than museums now to me.

I loved staying too with the Burgeses at Parkanaur. They were a very good-looking family, and although the children were still in the schoolroom there was always something going on, even if it was only cleaning eggs or picking raspberries. But they loved entertaining so there were always shoots in winter and tennis in summer. Among their neighbours who often came were the Stronges of Tynan and the Mulhollands of Ballyscullion. Sir Norman Stronge was Speaker of the House in the Stormont parliament and his daughters were my age. Sir Henry Mulholland, brother of Lord Dunleath, was chairman of the York Street Flax Spinning Company and had been Speaker until 1943. They were both brilliant shots; it was considered very bad form to shoot badly and wound birds so most of theirs died at once. I did not like seeing them killed but they did provide delicious and much needed additions to our still-rationed larders, and I loved the sounds and scents of the woods and bogs where we waited for the birds to come over. I also liked the attractive intelligent men! A wife or daughter often accompanied each gun to hold the spaniel or Labrador until a bird fell. The dogs adored shooting and waited quivering with excitement until told to retrieve. Even my Border terrier would get wild with excitement too at the sight of a gun-case; and of course watching first class shots one greatly admired their skill. These were all wild birds, and strong fliers, not at all easy to hit.[1]

The men were always charming to me, teasing and cracking jokes; one often heard words of wisdom and much country lore as well. I remember Sir Harry saying to me à propos of someone we both knew, 'We are funny people in Ulster you know; we like people to do well, but not too well!' I don't know why this stuck in my mind, but it did. He could chide one too, as when I made a cynical remark about something, and he said promptly 'Don't say that. You are much too pretty to say a thing like that.'

There was always a break for lunch, no boring sandwiches gobbled in the car as at syndicates nowadays, but a sit-down affair in the dining room, which at Parkanaur was almost a banqueting hall; game pie, treacle tart and Stilton cheese. Lord Caledon did not shoot but enjoyed parties so he often came for the lunch. His brother Lord Alexander of Tunis had been one of our most distinguished generals in the war, a most charming man … a real 'seigneur', who was at that time Governor General of Canada. Eric

---

1 Much later, on one historic occasion at Finnibrogue, a young man in the Rifle Brigade shot a wild duck which fell some way out in the lake. It was very cold, and nothing would persuade his dog to go in and retrieve it. Finally, to the amazement of all the other guns, he leapt into the lake, swam out, and retrieved the bird himself.

Lord Caledon never married and spent much of his time at his other house in England, or his London club. He was rather eccentric but delightful too. Once when we were walking round the kitchen garden at Tynan in a cold Ulster summer ... they were all keen and competitive gardeners ... I was blowing on my frozen fingers to warm them when he said 'Is your hand cold?' and took it and put it in his coat pocket, for which I was truly grateful. Caledon, a lovely Georgian house, is now lived in by his great-nephew the present Earl, which is good to know.

Caledon, Tynan, and Glaslough, the home of Sir Shane Leslie, author and eccentric, were adjacent properties like a clover leaf where one could walk from one to the other, though Glaslough was now in the republic. This area was all part of the Vale of the Black Pig, famous for its fertility from time immemorial. Tynan was no exception, and Sir Norman was justly proud of his trees and the beautiful lime walk. The present house was mostly Victorian Tudor Gothic remodelled on the 18th century house. It had a lovely library which opened onto the terrace where so many famous politicians from the Commonwealth and Empire had strolled, including Mrs. Ghandi, Mrs Pandit, Mr. Mackenzie-King of Canada and Mr Menzies of Australia.

Alas in 1978 Sir Norman, then 84 and his only son Jim were murdered there by the IRA, and the house with all its contents including a priceless collection of silver burnt over them. Lady Stronge, mercifully, had died some years before.

Few if any of the beautiful older wives in those days could cook, or even boil an egg, and by 1949 domestic servants were already becoming a thing of the past. Country girls had gone to work in industry in the towns during the war, where wages were higher and the work much harder, but there was also more for them to do in their free time; shops, cinemas, and bright lights. Taxes and death-duties continued and became enormous, inevitable no doubt to pay for the war; many sons and heirs had been killed and country house living had to be cut accordingly. In England staff had already gone, and we had all had to cook and clean since the war began; any staff we had at Witton had joined up for war work.

Before one large Sunday tennis party at Parkanaur I had offered to help by making a cake, and Christine ... Mrs Burges ... came too. She had never made a cake before, but we descended to the enormous kitchen hung with copper pots and pans of every size, and preceded to make a very good rich sticky ginger cake from a recipe I knew. It was quite easy because one put everything except the eggs and flour into a saucepan first and heated it till it was a runny mess of treacle, margarine and sugar ... butter was still rationed. Poor Christine stirred gloomily away at this saying 'I can't believe this will ever turn into a cake!'

It did however, and a very good one, but when we offered it to one young man at tea after the tennis he said crushingly, 'No thank you, I'd rather have the other one, it looks so much nicer.' Outraged, Christine and I cried at once 'But WE made this!' He was covered in confusion I am glad to say, quite unused to the cooking being done by the lady of the house. In fact she did later become a first-class cook, and took far more pains with it than I ever did.

In 1950 my sister Coralie became engaged to Robin Kinahan of the well known firm Lyle and Kinahan. He too had served through the war in France and Burma. Sir Milne and Aunt Jane were delighted, they were great friends of his parents. We all stayed at Conway for the wedding, and Sir Milne and Aunt Jane gave a great lunch party there for all the de Burgh and de Robeck relations who had come up from Kildare for the ceremony in Belfast Cathedral, of which Robin was already a churchwarden.

They also lent Coralie and Robin a cottage on the estate after they returned from their honeymoon until they found a house of their own at Mallusk. Sir Milne thought Robin, already a Councillor and prospective

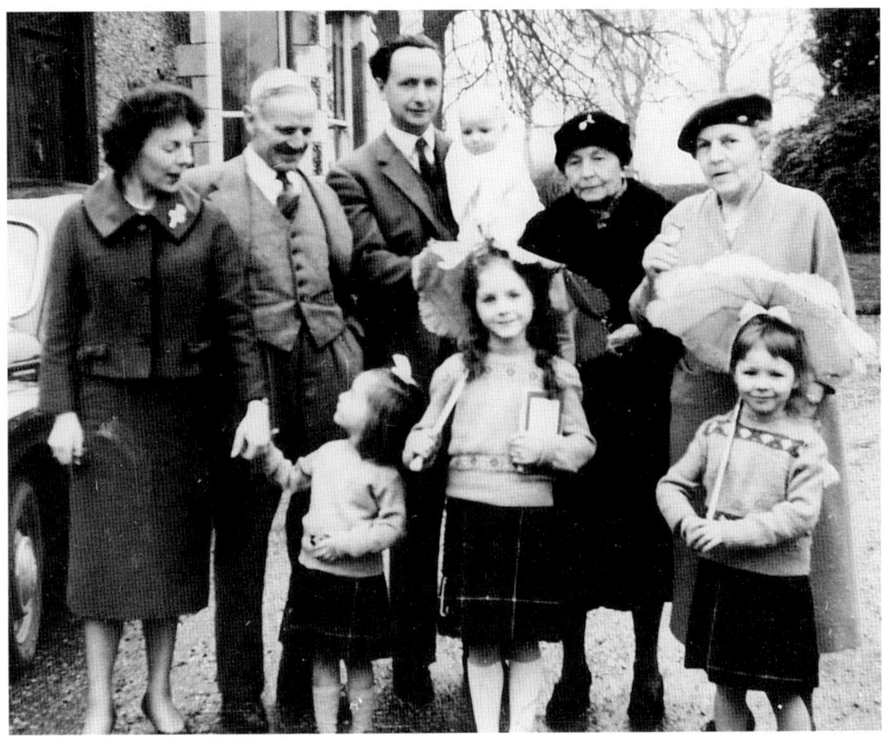

Danny Kinahan's first Christmas
Lydia de Burgh, my father, Robin with Danny, Aunt Jane, my mother.
In front: Vivi, Lulu and Emma Kinahan

M.P. would go far, and time has proved him right, for over the years Robin became High Sheriff of Belfast, then Lord Mayor, and finally Lord Lieutenant of the city. They have kept up their close connection with the cathedral since on many famous and family occasions, and two of their daughters, my beloved nieces, have been married there.

Sad to say Sir Milne died in 1952 aged 84, but he would have greatly approved of Robin's success. He had been such a kind, delightful host both to Coralie and me on many occasions, and after his death Conway was sold. All his daughters by then lived in England and although there were other Barbour relations none of them wanted to take on a place of that size and a way of life that was already fading into the past. After Conway became a hotel, the main house was destroyed by IRA bombs in the '70s, and modern buildings I believe stand in its place; I have never been back. I would much rather think of it and them all as I first saw it, and the haven of welcome it seemed to a sick, war-weary girl of nineteen so many years ago.

CHAPTER 9

LONDON

HAVING JUST TURNED sixteen when it began, I was twenty two when the war ended; but it was another year before it became possible to resume any study for a career. There was no time to be wasted for my parents could not afford to keep me in London after my father retired from managing the Dean and Chapter Estates.

While there my sister and I lived at the top of Pierce Synnott's house in Thurloe Square. Our flat though somewhat basic became the greatest fun. I studied opera which I loved though it was then totally unfashionable, until after three years it became, sadly, only too clear that although I had been endowed with a beautiful voice (and altogether too much temperament) the legacies of insomnia and other disabilities from my war work had left me bereft of the stamina and constitution essential for becoming a successful prima donna. It was a great disappointment that all my hard work singing and the cost of the training had been wasted, though knowledge, I later discovered, is seldom quite wasted. One just has to accept such things.

Fortunately I loved painting too, had always painted, and had been well taught even by governesses. One Swiss governess taught us little else but painting and French. So, on my father's advice, I went back to this, studying portrait painting with Sonia Mervyn R.P. She was an excellent painter and teacher and only took a few promising pupils. Quite soon I began to get commissions myself while still studying, and I also worked part time at the Tate gallery and the Victoria and Albert Museum to earn enough to keep going.

In those days one could get a fried herring and a baked potato at the V. and A. for six and a half old pence, about two and a half new pence now. It was also extremely interesting and I learnt much from working both there and at the Tate Gallery, surrounded by wonderful works of art of all periods and countries, not to mention the furniture and china.

Painting was then still looked on by most people I knew as simply a pleasant hobby for girls, rather like arranging flowers and doing tapestry.

All young ladies in the past had been expected to paint, play the piano and sew proficiently, but most of all they were expected to marry and marry suitably. The brief emancipation of the twenties and thirties had hardly percolated to Ireland or Scotland, but the second war drastically changed girls' lives. Many of us had carried out arduous, vital and often menial work in the armed and other services, living rough. High taxation, plus a real shortage of men because so many had been killed or damaged in the war, meant girls had to be able to support themselves.

The transition did not come easily. At first some thought life would go back to a pre-1939 way of living, but debutantes did now learn domestic science. This mostly meant a little housework, cooking and sewing, also typing after a fashion. To be seriously artistic or intellectual was an awful social handicap and one to be disguised at all costs.

My mother unfortunately could not stand brainless women. Having been married for so long before we were born and in a mainly masculine environment she did not much like women at all. Although a very feminine woman herself she encouraged us to be intelligent without explaining that we must also disguise the fact, and I alas was not intelligent enough to work this out for myself! My father had taught us to be resourceful and good with tools ... like axes. So it was distinctly bewildering to find, with peace, all this had to be suppressed. Young men did not like young ladies swinging axes and splitting logs, which they were often abysmal at doing themselves. To be a social success one had to become giddy, ornamental and feminine again. This actually required quite an effort, but it seems we were successful!

The outbreak of war in Korea barely five years after the end of the last, the second, world war, brought all this to a halt. The thought of yet another war, death, hardship and separation was appalling ... let alone rationing which was still going on and worse than ever. Many of those still kicking up their heels wisely decided to marry, and married happily. At this time there was no-one I wanted to marry. It could not truthfully be said there was no-one who wanted to marry me, but I was not well, and there was no-one with whom I might have been happy. I seemed to exert an irresistible attraction over men who were neurotic, morons, or wildly unstable ... some of them were very good looking; but I was too wary to marry them.

Meanwhile I oscillated happily between sixpenny herrings at the 'V. and A.' and lunch On Guard at St James's Palace.

Before the war and for some time after it I believe, officers in the Brigade of Guards when out of uniform in London were expected to wear bowler hats, bought from Herbert Johnston, and they were not allowed to carry anything but a well furled umbrella; not even the smallest parcel was permitted, no discreet package from Fribourg and Trier, Harrods, or Fortnum and Mason, and certainly nothing in a paper bag ... plastic in those days had not been invented. Wives could carry the parcels, or they could be taken in a taxi; but many shops still delivered, so people could have things sent. Fribourg and Trier sold exclusive snuffs and tobaccos, including heavenly- smelling squashy Turkish cigarettes called 'Abdulla,' and slim black Russian ones with gold tips. These were delivered by a spanking turnout of dark green carriage and pair of bay horses driven by an immaculate liveried coachman. Of course there also had to be someone at the other end to receive the parcels; a valet perhaps?

Buses were also forbidden territory to officers in the Brigade. They might not travel on a motor bus. This fact came to light for me when coming out of the theatre in Shaftsbury Avenue late one evening with Gillie and Richard Butler and another man, both in the Irish Guards. We were all in evening dress. It was drizzling, and there just were no taxis free. Suddenly Richard espied a number 14 bus and said: 'Look! Let's take that', so he and Gillie and I leapt nimbly on board to the amazement of the other man who was left stranded on the pavement. There was nothing he could do except break into a brisk trot which rapidly became a canter and catch up with us at the next stop.

'You should not have done that Richard!' he protested furiously, being two full years senior.

'I don't care' said Richard, 'I want dinner!'

Ties could also be a problem. One might not wear a Brigade tie after six in the evening. After that one was supposed to be wearing a dinner jacket and therefore a black tie. It was indeed another world!

Having no brothers, all these slightly absurd and delightful arrangements were wryly explained to me by admirers and friends as we strolled back from lunch at some popular watering hole like the Guard's club, to which all serving officers then had to be long. The club was still in Charles St. (Mayfair) with the Ladies' Annex situated firmly on the opposite side of the road. Shepherd's Market was just around the corner, and Trumper, the fashionable barber's shop, a few steps further away in Curzon St.

Trumper made two different kinds of 'hair lotion for gentlemen', ... called Isis and Euchris. One was for greasy hair and one for dry, I forget which was which, but one had a nice smell and the other did not. I discovered this when dancing in nightclubs. We often danced cheek to cheek ... then wildly daring! ... and my nose came just below my partners' hair. Unfortunately my favourite men all seemed to use the nasty one, so I complained, as occasionally a waft of the other would drift past on someone else. All I could do was to take protective action by drenching myself in Guerlain's 'Mitsouko' which proved a popular move. Scent ... it was never called perfume ... was just reappearing on the market after the long famine of the war, and I loved it. I remember my sister writing to a boyfriend serving in North Africa in a smart cavalry Regiment and we dabbed his letter liberally with the last of my mother's 1930 Chanel No. 5. It apparently still smelled nostalgically when it arrived months later in the middle of the desert battles, and everyone in the mess-tent from the Colonel down sniffed the air rapturously like old warhorses!

The Guard's Boat Club was at Maidenhead. Membership of this was not compulsory, but all who could afford to joined as it was a cool refreshing place to scull, play tennis, lunch and invite wives and lady-friends if one was stationed in London. The Boat Club Ball was one of the best parties of the season and invitations were eagerly sought. Coralie and I were asked in 1948 by a friend called Charles in the Scot's Guards, ('Puffin' to his colleagues). Ours was quite a large party and it should have been glamourous too because in between reels and foxtrots one took the club's boats out on the Thames in the moonlight ... only that night there was no moon, an oversight, no doubt. My current favourite escort was not there so I missed him, though that was better than him being therewith somebody else. All the boats had little engines because the Thames could be tricky, and Coralie and Anthony drifted away downstream.

By 2 a.m. the Ball was grinding to a halt and I was longing for my warm bed, but there was no sign of Coralie and Anthony. We waited and we waited. At about 4 a.m. the band went home and we were still waiting. Finally as dawn broke my sister and her partner straggled into view, damp, dishevelled and absolutely dripping with waterweed and every other sort of weed, exhausted and very cross.

It seems their engine had cut out some way down stream and there were no oars. They were quite near a weir so it was frightening as well. The only way they could get back was to pull the boat the whole way alongside the bank by hand from tuft to tuft of grass and rushes; or so they said, and I for one believed them. One look at Coralie's face dispelled any idea that it might have been fun! Clothes were still rationed and sad to say this had put paid to her beautiful dress, (made of priest's veiling bought in Naas), which had found itself frisking at so many fashionable night spots from the Queen Charlotte's Ball on.

I remember thinking 'Oh well, next year it will be better.' But there never was a next year ... for me anyway ... because very soon the Boat Club got into financial difficulties; it was very expensive and people could now go further afield at week-ends. Later it closed down altogether, and nothing is left now but sparse grass where it once stood, not even a hole in the ground where the swimming pool was; (it was always icy cold). Nearby residents walk their dogs there, and one more landmark of the old London season has disappeared.

Another feature of that London scene in summer after the war was still the flower 'girl' on the corner of Bond Street and Picadilly, where she sold buttonholes of violets, carnations and gardenias. Despite being desperately short of money I could seldom resist a gardenia with its exotic , almost cloying scent, and it would last for days in an egg cup on my dressing table. I think she too has disappeared and people do not buy posies for buttonholes any longer except for weddings? Nowadays she would be trampled under foot by uncomprehending crowds; but weird as all these customs now seem they did provide a living, and human contact, and links with the past as well.

One institution that did not come up to expectations was Rosa Lewis and the Cavendish Hotel ... famed for its randy lifestyle. Hearing that I had never been there my cousin Ralph Anstruther took me along one evening. This must have been in 1950, so not long before Rosa died, aged eighty-five. In fact I knew little about her as no book had yet been written of her life, and she was not of course mentioned in any of the memoirs of her great protégés, Sir William Eden, (father of Anthony) Lord Ribblesdale, of the famous 'Ancestor' painting, and others; the Cavendish was still not exactly respectable and too many of the habitués or their descendants, I suspect,were still alive.

Rosa was sitting in a chair by the fire in her little parlour on the right of the front door, with the devoted Edith[1] in attendance. The room was colourless and drab but the walls were plastered with photographs of her beloved 'boys' of bygone days ... very few women ... and she was surrounded by men, mostly of a very different type from those of her gilded past, but all hoping she would say something outrageous, or filthy! ... her language could be very fruity.

Rosa herself seemed slumped in thought, almost torpid. She had a typical peasant's face with strong, plain features and a beautiful skin. Even at eighty it was smooth and fair with hardly a line on it to show how hard she had worked, or the vast quantities of champagne she must have consumed; and everyone was still drinking champagne, but the whole place smelt fusty, and was shabby with age. Ralph introduced me and said:

'This is my cousin Lydia, from Ireland, Rosa,' and I smiled politely. For a bit nothing happened, then there was a sort of rumble, and 'Never did like Ireland!' said Rosa loudly. (Never did like girls much either I felt sure.) Everyone giggled hopefully.

'Which part of Ireland were you in?' I asked her. Another pause, 'Rockingham,' she said firmly, 'Rockingham. Never did like Ireland'.

---

[1] Rosa's companion of later years. As a footnote to the above it should perhaps also be said that many very respectable people stayed at the Cavendish too.

Now I was really stumped ... I knew the Stafford-King-Harmans who owned Rockingham; I very nearly blurted out 'What were you doing there?' but realised in time it might be a tactless question! In fact it was probably before the 1914 war and she was over there catering and cooking for some Vice-Regal shooting party on a grand scale ... I do not think Rosa's set- up would have cut much ice with the Irish of any sort, especially the servants; but she might have been offended. By now, for her, fact was often shrouded in fantasy; and she was an awful snob; which was probably why she did not like Ireland.

She did not speak again and no doubt went on ruminating about Rockingham; like many very old people her mind was quite clear about the distant past. We did not stay long, and alas I thought she was a rather dreadful old woman, but interesting because she was unique.

I am sure the great charm she held for rich men of the Victorian days was that she reminded them of their nannies. Children of that generation hardly saw their parents ... dazzling creatures perpetually away at house parties or in London, who had little to do with bringing up the children. It was Nanny ... and nursery maids ... who ran the children's lives; often kind, but strict, so that they knew just where they were.

'Now Master Robert, eat up that pudding or you'll never be big and strong,' ... 'have you cleaned your teeth yet?' ... 'sat on your pot?' 'Handsome is what handsome does' was another dictum, 'tell tale tit, your tongue shall be split!' and so forth. She also settled all squabbles, and dosed them with castor oil when necessary. 'NOW whose Nanny's handsome little boy!' would be the final accolade. Sometimes she provided the only real affection and stability the children received.

I think Rosa performed the same functions for many men when grown-up, or grown-old, probably providing them with a bottle of champagne (usually put on the bill of the most nouveau-riche man staying at the Cavendish), good food, (a woman if wanted,) and even occasionally still a good dose. She could also be really kind; Lord R., a devoted father and husband at home, virtually lived there after the tragic deaths of his wife and later, in the 1914–18 war, his two sons.

Both the Weymouths obviously loved her before and after the last war, and so did their daughter Caroline of the incredibly long legs and little flower-like face, who was more my contemporary. But Rosa's world really ended in 1918 with that war, when ironically, respectability at which she had so often jeered, went out of the window.

Here I think a point should be made about the morals and mores of those considered 'fast' in Edwardian days when most well-bred girls were married straight from the schoolroom at eighteen or less, knowing nothing at all about sex and often not in love with their husbands. Marriages were planned for suitability. Quite often this was a success, but the girl usually found herself having a baby within the first year, with no anaesthetics or modern surgery, and probably three or four more in the next six years as there were few contraceptives either. Death in childbirth was also common. I suspect to some wives it was almost a relief if their husbands had women friends elsewhere provided of course that they were not made to look foolish or neglected. Most husbands were careful not to do this and the framework of the marriage and family remained intact. The unwritten law was that the man must never contract syphilis, for which there was no cure, and never bring it home to his wife. It was then incurable and a pretty dreadful death. Men for their part expected their wives to be virtuous, certainly until they had produced a legitimate heir or two. Given the circumstances of those days does this seem such hypocrisy? I think not, though I personally believe in morals. Even in 1950 however I can remember overhearing a young man I rather liked saying that when he married it would be for dynastic reasons! I thought this sounded both pompous and chilling, and went off him fast.

I left London in March 1953 to help my parents with moving back to Ireland and selling our lovely but no longer viable home at Witton. I wanted to live in Ireland too, and hoped to continue painting though my work was as yet unknown there.

CHAPTER 10

COUNTY DOWN

THE MOVE TO IRELAND PROVED a formidable task. Witton was rather a big house in a beautiful but remote part of County Durham where it seemed no-one wanted to live, so we had not been able to sell it by 1953, and much of our lovely furniture had to be sold instead to raise badly needed money. There was no interest at all then in antiques ... people thought they could build a new world with new things; so alas, it was all sold for a song.

It was chance that brought us to Count Down. My sister, already married to Robin Kinahan, was living at Mallusk, then a small old mill village, when she met Colonel Desmond Forde at a party and heard that he had a pretty Regency house to let in his demesne; and so it was that we came to Seaforde, and I grew to love it.

The village takes its name from the Forde family who owned much of the surrounding land, had rebuilt the church and given much to it. The original big house had burnt down and no picture of it remains; the present one was built in 1816, and is surrounded by beautiful woods and trees of the demesne which helps to make Seaforde such a pretty village, with the Mountains of Mourne in the distance.

Although small, in 1953 it still had a post office, an excellent butcher's shop, a blacksmith's forge, and two grocery shops one of which sold everything from bacon and cheese to gumboots and cartridges. Mr Boyd was also the undertaker. So Seaforde was really quite self-contained. It had of course its own Clergyman, and a Policeman. Within half a mile were the only foxhound kennels in Ulster. Our house, the Lodge, was just a short distance away up a drive, and looked straight out onto the Mournes.

County Down was almost unknown to me then. I do remember one outing to Downpatrick races just after the war when petrol was still in very short supply. I went down by train with Tony Clark (later Sir George), Teddy Archdale (now Sir Edward) and his sister Patty, and it puffed its way through the beautiful countryside via the Loop almost to the racecourse. The sun shone, the gorse was in full bloom, and the grass was like a green velvet carpet as we sat about on rugs eating our picnic lunch. Little did I think that I would soon be spending much of my life nearby, but I would have been happy to know it.

After we had moved in at Seaforde, no easy task with very old parents, Downpatrick races was one of the first social events that I went to. The course, though beautifully situated amongst rolling hills, is not an easy one for horses and slightly resembles a switchback. It was critically short of money then, and some years later the committee met to discuss repairs to the grandstands which were alleged to be somewhat unsafe.

'Nothing has been done to them for years,' sighed one of the stewards.

'Ah now, sorr' said a groundsman indignantly, 'Didn't I put two good new planks into them only last year, so I did.'

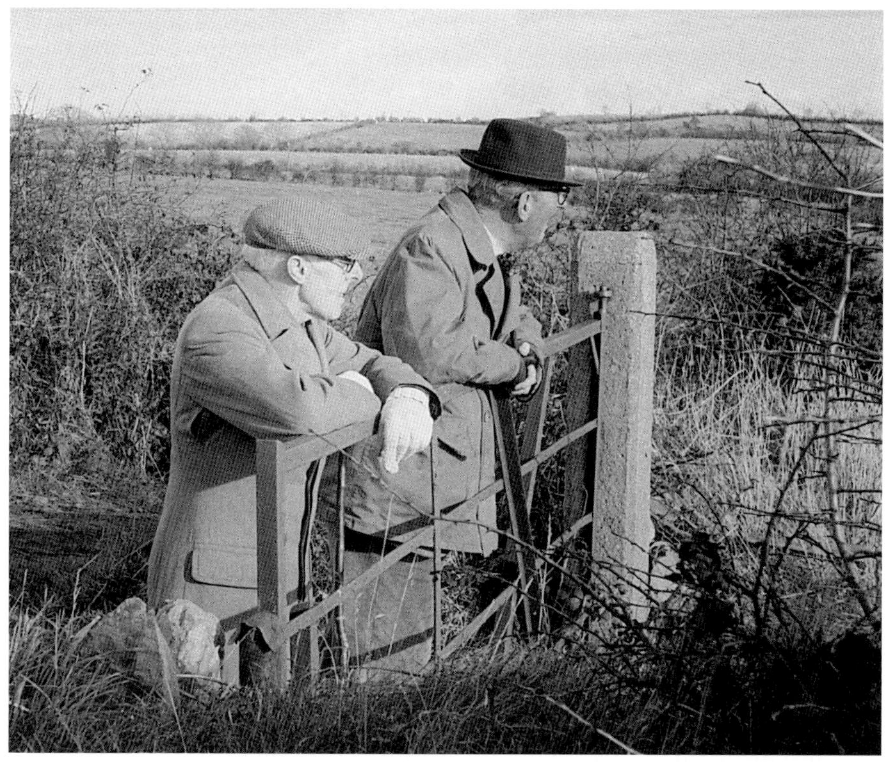

Lieutenant Commander Kenneth Kirkpatrick and Lieutenant Colonel Desmond Forde, watching hounds

Much more than planks have been added now and the racecourse continues to flourish, looking very smart indeed, but sad to say many of the old familiar faces are no longer with us.

It was then still the fashion to wear smart country clothes racing, at least in the members' enclosure; it was a social occasion. One sat about on shooting sticks or on the steps, and everyone from round about except

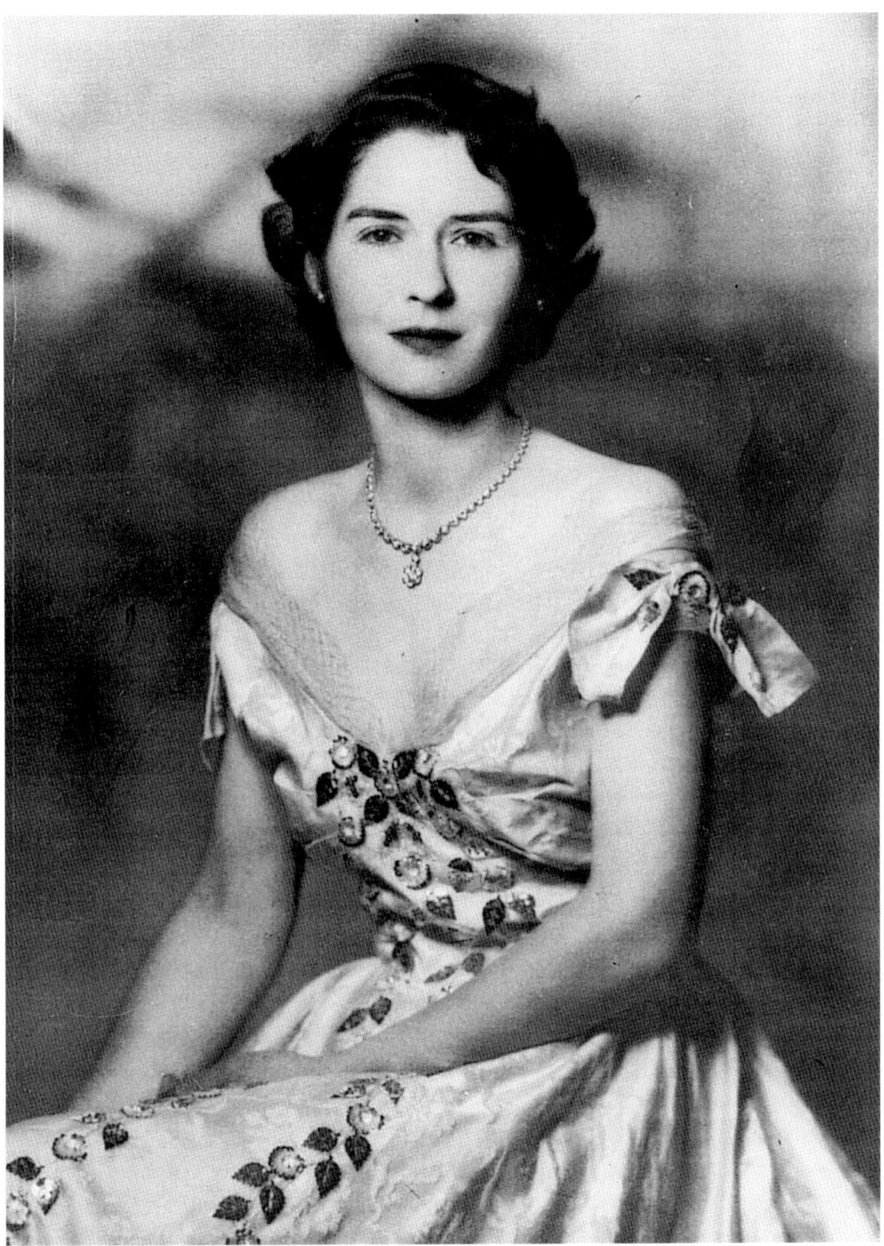

Clodagh, Countess of Roden, by kind permission of her son, the present Earl

those who absolutely loathed horses came there, often from across the border. Among the stewards then were Commander Kenneth Kirkpatrick of Church Hill, formerly Master of the Staghounds, Colonel Perceval-Maxwell of Finnebrogue, Sir Roland Nugent of Portaferry House, and Colonel Forde; also much younger Lord Dunleath, despite suffering seriously from hay-fever. I did not know them all then but they later became friends.

One I did know was Lady Roden, who was very beautiful, because she came from Kildare. Her father was 'Cub' Kennedy who bred the 'Tetrarch', a famous Derby winner, and for a long time the fastest, whose bloodlines run in most thoroughbreds racing today. Bishopscourt, where the Kennedys lived, was very near my father's home Oldtown, and he sometimes used to push Clodagh about in her pram when he was a Midshipman, because she was such a pretty baby. Her Husband, Lord Roden, of Bryansford, was also in the Navy.

Downpatrick is the county town and St. Patrick is said to be buried there. It still has some beautiful Georgian buildings, which are now being restored. Sad to say many others were destroyed in the sixties which must surely rival 'L'Époque de Mauvais Gout' in France during the last century. I remember little shops with bow windows and small, curved panes of glass in Irish Street, and they have all gone. Besides the Cathedral, the Court House, the Downe Hunt rooms and the Alms Houses opposite are beautiful; the old gaol has been converted now into an excellent museum ... a really great piece of renovation. The Victorian Assembly Rooms are now an art centre and theatre where there are many new facilities.

One slightly less salubrious state of affairs in those days was at the General Post Office, the main one for the district. Here, at least five or six large stray mongrel dogs were inclined to use it as a kennel during the day. It was pleasantly heated, so many a morning when the doors opened in they rushed and spread themselves comfortably about the floor; and the same thing happened after the lunch break.

Unfortunately during the mating season, which seemed to go on for months, copulation took place as well, and because there were always more dogs than bitches several ferocious fights were sometimes in progress too. This made simple matters like buying a stamp quite hazardous. The Post office staff, safely entrenched behind the counter, were always (and still are) most helpful. The problem was how to reach them!

Now all that has changed, the new building has dog-proof doors, and since the license for dogs went up from five shillings to five pounds all dogs have vanished from the scene. Unfortunately it is still quite difficult to buy a stamp even in 1990 ... so much else being dispensed there as well.

There were some splendid characters about in Downpatrick too but sad to say they are rapidly dying out. I met one not so long ago when I was invigilating as a member for the Down Art Society, at the annual exhibition in the Library.

I was sitting there twiddling my thumbs together with an accomplished colleague from Portaferry, when in walked a rather drunken man and sat down beside us. He was fairly old but well set-up, wearing good tweeds, and clearly ready for a bit of chat. My colleague looked somewhat taken aback but I have always found the best routine with drunken men is to behave as if they were sober ... when possible ... and it was.

The conversation went something like this:
Him, 'You're a good-looking girl,[1] would you care for a jar?' His pockets were bulging with cans of beer. 'No, no', I said , 'We are on duty you know. Not allowed to drink on duty!'

He then started asking riddles. I forget what the first was but I did not know the answer, so I said 'Do you mean to tell me you don't know that!' 'Of course I know, 'said he. 'Well then, why are you asking me!' I replied. 'Cheeky bitch!' said he, slapping his thigh with delight. My lady colleague was looking more and more taken aback.

This could have gone on for ages but fortunately other people came in, and he went off, beer cans clanking. He had remarkably fine hands, I had noticed, and well kept. An interesting character.

Formerly Downpatrick was surrounded by marshes ... it still is in very wet weather ... which belonged to the Dunleath and Perceval-Maxwell families. There was a great concentration of bird-life on these marshes, and once or twice a year there were tremendous duck and wild-geese shoots, when one had to lie almost up to the neck in icy water before dawn, waiting for the flights to come in. I never actually took part any of these. It was altogether too cold, and I am rather fond of ducks; but later, when the marshes were drained ... more or less ... their habitat was destroyed and many of the rare birds have ceased to come.

Gardening now became for me a new interest, but hard work. The gardens at Witton had been lovely and already well established when we bought it, but the Lodge had been unoccupied for some years and the garden was reverting to jungle. Altogether there were 17 acres, at least two of them garden. We had not had a gardener since the war, and my mother was no longer able for it, so my father and I set to work. Much of it was lawns, but we had always cut these ourselves at Witton because my father was afraid of the gardener wrecking the motor mowers, and we had brought these over with us. At the big house, the Forde's, which had acres of lovely lawn, I seem to remember the machines there were still drawn by a pony wearing leather lawn boots, so that it did not leave marks.

---

[1] I was about 60!

We were surrounded by famous gardens and arboretums at Seaforde. The climate was much milder than in the North East of England, and rare and lovely shrubs and trees flourished. Castlewellan was the nearest then and a fine example of both. It still belonged to the Annesleys and had been planted and planned by them in the mid-nineteenth century on the hills sloping away from the Castle. The trees planted by the fourth Earl were now in their prime, with glimpses of the sea in the distance. This interest in landscape gardening continued in the family, and at the time we arrived Gerald Annesley was the occupant. He was a tremendous expert on trees and shrubs, especially rare rhododendrons which grew to enormous and spectacular size there. He had a reputation for being wild, but could also be great fun. His younger daughter, Margaret, had been a friend of ours in London and was back at Castlewellan in 1953.

Gerald was the nephew of Frank, the 6th earl, who had been killed flying on active service in 1915; then a Lieut. in the Royal Naval Reserve he had transferred to the Royal Flying Corps despite having only one eye. He had lost the other in a wild party when up at Cambridge some years before. I was asked to paint a posthumous portrait of him quite recently for the Royal County Down Golf Club of which he had been president, but there was only an old blurred photograph of him, not easy to work from. He was small and looked fun, but I could not make out why his eyes did not match, until his great-nephew who had never seen him either, enlightened me.

After Frank's death the estate went to his sister Lady Mabel, Gerald's mother, whose husband had also died. She resumed the name of Annesley and still lived there in a separate part of the house looking over the side terrace. She was a considerable expert on Coptic art, and both drew and wrote poetry very well herself. I wished I had known then that I was going to paint 'Frank' as I could have asked her about him; she was small and charming too.

Half way up the stairs to the main floor at Castlewellan there stood a ancient and ferocious suit of Japanese armour, an extraordinary affair of steel and woven straw with a very fierce expression. Encountering this for the first time my border terrier who came everywhere with me was quite taken aback. He sniffed all round it suspiciously, and then to my consternation spent a simply enormous penny on it! 'Oh! That's how I've always ALWAYS felt about it!' cried one of the family, who happened to be looking down.

Gerald sold Castlewellan in 1965 after he married his third wife, whom much later I also painted; ('I want you to paint her' he said, 'because she is the best wife I have had'!) Castlewellan is now in the good hands of the Ministry of Agriculture, forestry department, and two water colours of it which I also painted, I later sold to friends.

It was no doubt because of the Annesley connection that Hugh Armitage Moore and his wife Janie had made the beautiful garden at Rowallane some miles away. Hugh was, I think, the nephew of another Priscilla, Countess of Annesley, and obviously shared their love of gardens. He and his wife were very old by the time we came to County Down but I had met them at Conway during the war. Sad to say they had no children, so Rowallane was left to the National Trust.

How much one could write about those houses I knew and the highly entertaining people who lived in them, quite apart from the sometimes hilarious parties. But this is a serious book! So I must try to limit it now to those whom I painted as well.

Two portraits which were not much fun were the Headforts in County Meath where there was also a famous garden and arboretum, planted by Lord Headfort's father. These portraits were to be life size and full length, to fill enormous niches in the ballroom plaster-work; all the other niches were already full. The Headforts themselves were in late middle age, and poor Terry suffered from muscular dystrophy and could hardly walk, much less get into his former full-dress cavalry uniform in which he wished to be painted. Elsie, his wife, an Australian, at nearly sixty was not the best age for being painted. However this did not worry her at all; she just said firmly 'Now my dear, I want you to make me look twenty years younger and two stone lighter;' she also wanted her purple satin dress to be done as pink.

All this was some time before I painted the Queen, and I was rather young so did not like to protest. I needed the money, (which was not to be much ... some friends do exploit one) and anyway people want to look their best if possible. Elsie also wanted her two King Charles spaniels in the picture, and Terry looking twenty years younger to match. Fortunately he had a good photograph of himself at that age.

Being so large the portraits took a long time to paint and due to the above- mentioned problems were not ideal, though afterwards when people remarked tactlessly 'I say, she has made you look young!' Elsie always said 'Yes. That is just what I wanted.' I hated the pink dress but the spaniels were good. Apart from these trials the time passed pleasantly, and a great mutual friend Betty Musgrave, was staying there too. The main block of the house at Headfort was already let to a boy's preparatory school to which many of our friends and relations went, including my de Burgh cousins from Oldtown. The Headforts themselves lived in a wing in Summer, and in Australia in winter. We played all the Beethoven symphonies on the radiogram while I painted, and Elsie sat every morning. Then in the afternoon Terry liked to take me for a walk through the lovely demesne, he partly in his wheelchair, and partly on two sticks. He was extremely knowledgable and interesting about all trees and shrubs, but a problems for me because he was tall and heavy, and needed a lot of support or he fell over. This happened once on the island where his father was buried, and in no way could I heave him back onto his feet. I had to race off and find a gardener to help.

Their portraits still flourish in the ballroom which is the school assembly hall, but I believe the great gardens are long since overgrown. Since then I have always been strong minded enough to say "no" if I think the results will not be good.

It also made painting the Queen, later, who was a marvellous model, seem positively easy!

CHAPTER 11

MORE COUNTY DOWN

IN 1954 WHEN THERE SEEMED little hope of making a career painting in Northern Ireland I had the amazing good fortune to be asked to paint H.R.H. the Duchess of Gloucester, now Princess Alice; and this led to my painting H.M. the Queen. Of the sittings for these wonderful commissions at York House and Buckingham Palace, and later the Princess Royal at St James's Palace, I have already written at length in 'Lydia's Story'.

My parents needless to say were even more thrilled than I over these ... I still had to DO them! And before writing more it is necessary to put them into context with my life as it was at that time, which was not entirely a bed of roses ... or even rhododendrons.

The Lodge, our house, was little smaller than Witton and lacked the central heating which they were used to. With shortage of money and increasing infirmity as well as all the changes of post-war life my parents were quite unable to cope with only a daily help for three hours, so caring for them became my top priority. Well able to cope with hard work and shortages of money in their youth they hated old age and failing mentally and physically; and this was very depressing to see. Of this I have also written elsewhere. In spite of this both parents lived to be eighty seven but the problems for an unmarried daughter in those days are now very well known. They came of a strong generation when to survive childhood was an achievement even in grander families, and to survive two world wars even more so ... three including the Boer War (my Campbell grandmother wept for two days, it seems, when income-tax went up two pence in the pound after that, she thought they were ruined!) But it was very difficult for me then at the peak of my career which was hard work in itself, being physically and emotionally drained coping with everyday things at home, quite apart from matrimonial dramas of my own. My engagement to be married had been broken off only weeks before the wedding and a few months before I painted the Queen. If I had been stronger it might have been easier. However battle on one must.

I painted the Duchess of Gloucester at York House, St. James's Palace, and she was a charming model, despite considerable apprehension on both our parts! I had never painted without full-time sittings before and I knew she would never have time for that. She had seldom been painted at all and in middle age rather dreaded the prospect; and of course we had never met. For the first time I used photographs as well.

Fortunately it turned out a good likeness despite unsolicited advice from family and friends! I already knew St. James's palace quite well because Caroline Lascelles, whose father was Private Secretary to King George V1 and later the Queen, also lived there and was a great friend who often played my accompaniments when I was singing. I also loved lunching On Guard, as aforementioned, with friends who were Officers of the Guard on duty. (Girls were not invited to dinner.) In all the Royal households where I have painted everyday life is quite informal, once one has the entrée. Good manners, punctuality and efficiency are the order of the day, as they had always been for me at home. If one has the privilege of working there one respects it accordingly, and I do greatly despise people who abuse it for notoriety or money.

Her Royal Highness, daughter of the Duke of Buccleugh, has deep sapphire blue eyes and for the portrait she was wearing a crinoline dress of mushroom coloured tulle, with a splendid tiara and necklace. These jewels were by far the most difficult for me to paint, but proved excellent experience for when I came to paint the Queen the following year.

Quite apart from being chosen over many well-known, older, and established artists, painting the Sovereign must be the painter's accolade. The Queen was of course the ideal subject, young, beautiful and newly crowned. She is also serene, exceptionally interesting to talk to, and fun. As her Private Secretary Colonel Martin Charteris told me when arranging the sittings 'You will find her absolutely enchanting' ... which I did. The two official portraits which I painted of her, one three-quarters length in evening dress without a tiara, the second a half-length wearing the Imperial State Crown and coronation robes, are still among my very best works. (This is not just because she is Queen, but because it is very seldom that one gets a chance to paint someone in lovely clothes and jewels, who although young and beautiful also has great character, wide knowledge and interests. In a full length or a three-quarters length too there is far more scope with the pose; the play of light and shade on robes, and background interest so essential for a good picture. One really cannot produce a beautiful Titian or Van Dyke- type portrait of some person wearing an old shirt and jeans.

These paintings, especially those of the Queen, received worldwide publicity and acclaim. They were a huge boost to my morale, also to my career; (had they not been good they would have been just the reverse.) Many people naturally had not heard of me before, and some friends and relations who had looked on painting as a mere hobby hardly knew what to make of it. But it also meant having to learn at an early age how to deal with the press, photographers, public duties and speeches, though the two latter I had been brought up to do. It was not easy; I was still greatly occupied looking after my parents who needed much help, and they had been so good to us as children I felt I must continue to do so. Combining all this with rushing about painting was very tiring and insomnia became even more of a problem.

Fortunately many of the portraits I painted in the early '60s were of local people – the Fordes, the three little Blair girls, the Reas of Craigduff and others of whom I have already written.

Another sitter with a splendid garden was Henry Dunleath. He had married Dorinda Percival, already a friend of mine whose mother came from Co Tyrone. Like mine, Henry's parents had been quite old when he was born, and equally strict. They had greatly developed the gardens and planting at Ballywalter over the years and as at Mountstewart nearby huge rhododendrons and rare Chinese and South American trees flourished in the acid soil and mild County Down climate which they love.

I painted Henry soon after he and Dorinda were married. It was my wedding present to them both, and although only a small head it turned out very well, catching much of his vigour and tension. He was young and good-looking, but had never sat for his portrait before. Some of my

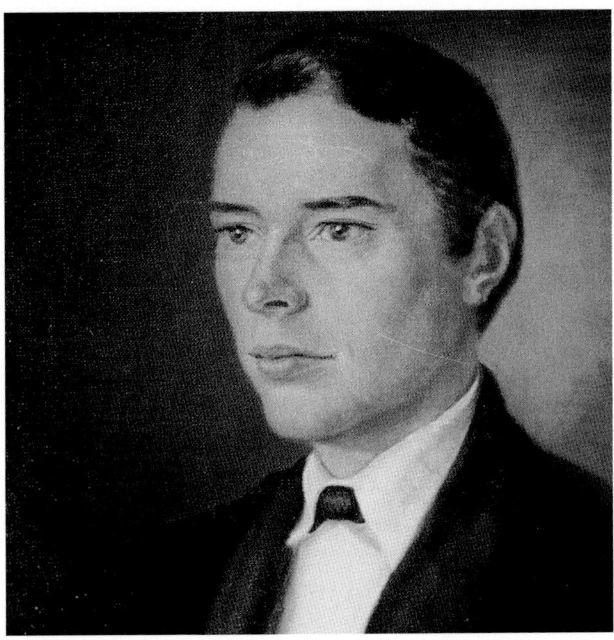

Lydia's painting of Henry as he really looked, 1963

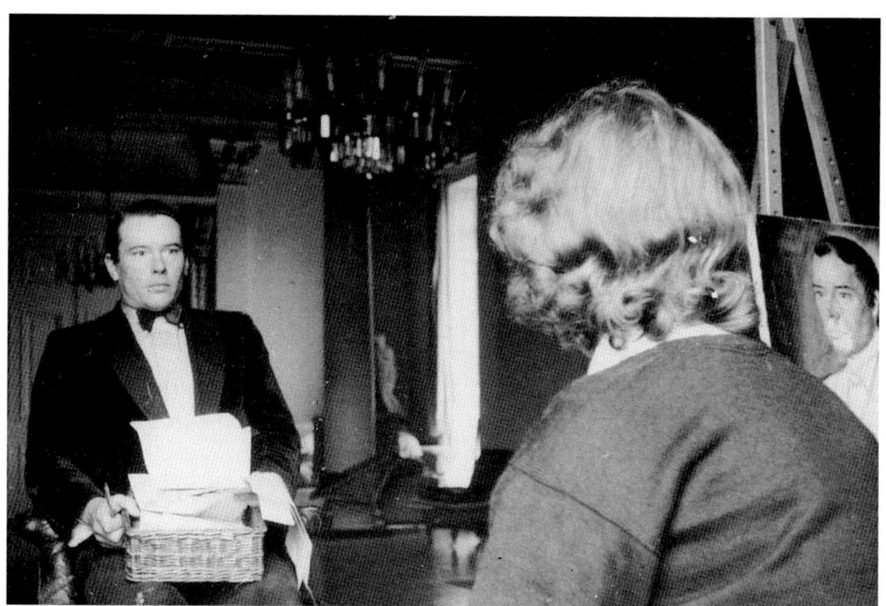

Problems of an artist! Henry Dunleath looking most unatural

photographs of him give some idea of the process one frequently goes through getting people to look natural! But it was fun, and they asked me to paint a companion portrait of Dorinda as well. This was less successful because I was going through a phase of blinding headaches, and she was draped in a blue velvet bedspread. Although always beautifully dressed, nothing else she had and that we could agree on seemed to look quite right; I am not sure that the bedspread did either! But she looked very pretty.

I always love staying there and they have been wonderful friends, especially Dorinda. Sometimes in summer we would wander out after dinner just to enjoy the garden and smell some glorious flower like *Rhododendron dalhousii* with its ravishing scent, tucked away in a sheltered shrubbery. Henry himself was more interested in vintage cars, trains and organs on which subjects he was a considerable expert. If he was asked the name of some shrub which he had forgotten he made up an immensely long imaginary Latin one, which was usually received with respectful admiration while Dorinda and I tried hard to keep straight faces. There were also rare magnolias, one of which had a powerful smell and we could never decide of what it reminded us. One night when there was some eminent professor, not a botanist, staying, we were all sniffing away at it our noses covered with pollen when suddenly it came to me; 'I know! It smells of antiflogistine', I exclaimed. 'That's it!' they cried, all of us could remember suffering from boiling antiflogistine poultices being clamped to our chests in childhood when ill. I had not thought of it for years… is it ever used now, I wonder?

There were two or three organs of great antiquity in the house at Ballywalter and usually several more lying carefully arranged in pieces in the stables, on tables, waiting for Henry to assemble. Anyone else who touched them was severely admonished.

Two of the stables in the corner were given over to Dorinda for her horses. She is the president of the Half- Bred Horse Breeder's Society and her great interest is in breeding prizewinning hunters, especially from the same bloodlines with which Henry's mother had been very successful. The current mare was 'Selina' who had a mind of her own and did not always fancy the stallions she was sent to. One spring, in order to make sure she was in foal Dorinda decided to take her to visit a nearby stallion. If 'Selina' was in foal she would evince no interest at all in him; if not, she would be returned to her lawful husband to be covered again.

This stallion was a champion Clydesdale which, we were told, lived with his owner in a clump of bushes on a disused airfield. Dorinda and I made our way over there towing 'Selina' on a rope. The bushes looked impenetrable, like the thicket round the Sleeping Beauty. After a careful circuit we found a way in, and at the far end of the clearing a small shed like a henhouse began to snort loudly and heave up and down. At the other end there was a sort of ruined tower. We all three approached this tower. On the door was a large 'Winnie the Pooh' type notice saying 'Away till

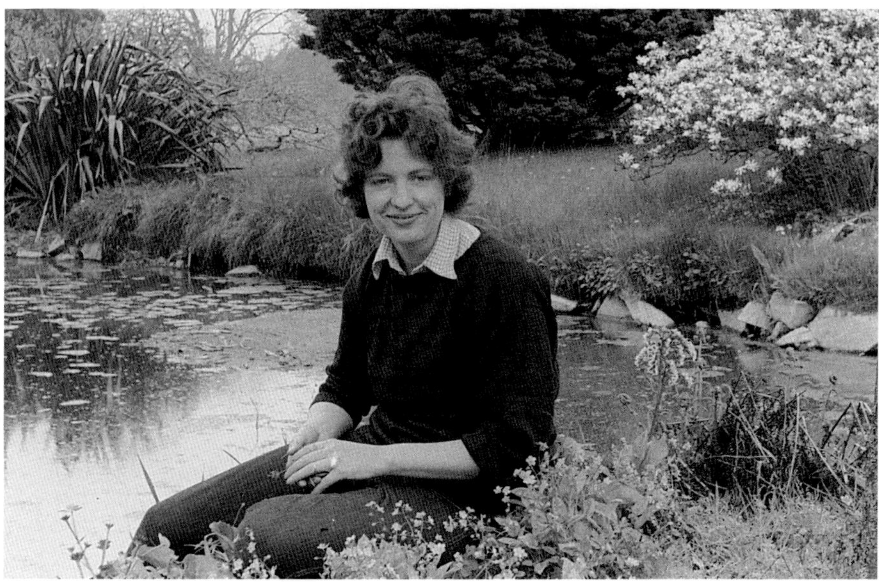

Dorinda Dunleath, Ballywalter

Friday. Don't knock unless you want an answer'. We studied this doubtfully. It was not Friday, but we did want an answer, so risked a knock. Nothing happened, except renewed snorts from the henhouse. At the third knock an elderly head sprouting an inch of beard stuck out of an upper window.

On seeing 'Selina' the owner came down, and Dorinda explained our mission. We all trooped over to the henhouse, out of which was led a simply enormous carthorse with huge flowing white fetlocks and a long white face with one blue eye and one brown, prancing wildly. Dorinda and I backed protectively round 'Selina', who nonchalantly munched a straw and gazed into the distance. We had our answer, she was not interested; but the civilities had to be observed. We loudly praised the beauty of the stallion ... it had won many prizes ... and the size of its feet as it galumphed around us.

'Aye', said the owner, 'They're great feet, and I get a' his shoes med in Glasgow!' We were duly impressed. To have left Scotland several years ago and still to have his shoes made there seemed luxury indeed; like getting one's hunting boots made by Tom Hall at Tattersall's in the old days. After a suitable exchange of compliments, mostly repetition, we towed the clearly pregnant 'Selina' away, trying hard not to collapse with laughter, while the owner strove to insinuate the sadly disappointed champion back into his henhouse.

Staying at Ballywalter one met a wide variety of interesting people, famous organ builders, clock experts, botanists, railway and motor connoisseurs, intermingled with mutual friends of a more ordinary kind. Sometimes I wondered if any of them realised that after the retirement of Mrs. Clarke Dorinda did all the cooking herself. Too many people think that if one lives in a very big house there is still a large unseen army of servants, which is not so.

◆

While writing this chapter Henry has tragically died, too young, at fifty-nine and others more erudite than I will write of his public work and enormous knowledge in many fields, particularly organs, about which he was one of the great experts in Europe, especially those of the eighteenth century. His interest in vintage cars, steam trains and politics was great, and he took an active part in the House of Lords. However because they are such special friends I feel someone should also record what fun he could be. Nothing one ever did with Henry was ordinary. On one occasion a party of Ulster steam train enthusiasts went to India to sample the rolling stock; wives went too. Everyone got awful tummy trouble except the two Old Etonians, Raymond O'Neill and Henry Dunleath. (This may be a backhanded compliment to Etonian food in wartime.)

Agra was then a great centre for trains as well as the Taj Mahal which they also viewed, one lady being so ill she was borne to see the latter on a stretcher.

Next day Dorinda went off to look at some of the charming but dilapidated Colonial bungalows in Cantonment Road, and Henry went off in a trishaw, a rickshaw attached to a tricycle. He decided it would be interesting to know how much manpower it took to propel the trishaw, and eventually managed to persuade the little man riding it to change places with him.

Henry was still pedalling happily back towards the hotel ... it is a very flat road ... with the little man sitting anxiously in the passenger seat behind, when the man became highly agitated and indicated in Hindi that Henry must stop and resume his seat. Henry could not think why, but it eventually transpired that it would entail awful lack of face if the other rickshaw men at the hotel saw this little man being pedalled by Henry. It would imply that he was not good enough. He told me himself of another time when he was about to drive home after a Down Hunt dinner in Downpatrick, wearing full Hunt evening dress with tail-coat, only to discover that the gears of his car had jammed ... it was not one of the vintage ones ... and it would only go in reverse. Nothing daunted he set off to drive the thirty miles to Ballywalter backwards. This proved taxing in the extreme given the circumstances, and when he reached the middle of Newtownards he was so tired he stopped for a rest, leant up against the door and promptly went to sleep.

The next thing he knew he was lying on his back in the gutter. Two large suspicious policemen were looking down at him with a 'Ho, Ho, what have we here?' sort of expression. They had opened the door and he had fallen out. Henry retrieved himself from the gutter and explained how he was driving home to Ballywalter and had stopped for a rest.

'Hm, hm,' said the policemen, 'Then why is it the car is now pointing towards Belfast?'

'Because you see, officer, as I was explaining, I am driving it backwards!' said Henry. Total disbelief on the part of the Police officers.

It is his vigour, good looks, and flashing smile that will be so much missed, and the fun we all had. Dorinda has always supported him in everything he did whether it was studying pollution in Poland or entertaining non-English speaking Chinese botanists at Ballywalter, though I doubt if he ever realised how much work it all entailed for her.

CHAPTER 12

PAINTINGS

ROYAL AND OTHERWISE

AS COUNTY DOWN IS NOT the easiest place to come for sittings I often stay with the people I am painting. This is almost always enjoyable ... for me at least; occasionally I already know them, but with strangers I must have some sittings. Most people are modest about their appearance and adept at concealing their personalities; but this is just what I need to discover, otherwise they will get a bland painted photograph which tells nothing of the real person. Sometimes there is nothing behind the façade, but rarely.

I do like people and find them interesting in whatever walk of life or country they may live. The problem with the British is getting them to wear interesting clothes. I have had to paint, inwardly kicking and screaming, at least twenty-five open-necked pale blue shirts in a traditional manner, when portraits of this kind should, I feel, be painted in a more modern idiom. The same goes for pin-striped suits. But most people want to look conventional wearing casual clothes; a contradiction in terms.

Bishops of course are ideal subjects ... beautiful flowing robes with bright dashes of colour. My first bishop, George Quin of Down and Dromore, watched with great amusement while I riffled through his wardrobe; I was quite carried away, torn between his purple cassock, and a red one with snowy white surplice and masses of frills. I then rushed round all the bedrooms looking for one with suitable light where I could also leave my paints and make a mess.

When we got downstairs his wife Norah, who had been away at a meeting, asked him: 'How are you getting on, dear?' 'Oh very well', replied the Bishop, 'We've tried out all the bedrooms and most of my clothes; I had no idea painting could be such fun!'

Lord mayors, admirals and generals can also be fun to paint ... no riffling through the wardrobes there. But give me a Nureyev with that marvellous face, beautiful but fraught, and such panache and glamour – he adored exotic clothes. I could paint a subject like that for ever.

Fortunately I can still fall back on Indians in brilliant saris or turbans, Thais in gleaming silks, African tribesmen, or even a spectacular beggar. They are quite uninhibited. Unfortunately they seldom have sixpence between them and would never be able to buy a painting; I pay them instead, hoping that one day some discerning collector will realise that many of these are my greatest pictures.

Meanwhile I continue with the conventional portraits which are what most people want. They are my bread and butter. I understand very well the apprehension most people feel about being painted. They do not quite know what they will get, though I insist on them seeing my work first, and they are afraid they will be jeered at by their 'friends'. They are also worried that it may all go on for too long. I am worried about this too. One famous artist painting official portraits of King George V1 and Queen Elizabeth managed to spend most of the war at Windsor Castle, which was the cause of some dismay.

I did not stay at Buckingham Palace when painting the Queen because my great friends the Summersons lent me their comfortable flat at Westminster, but I loved working there. It was a step back into the civilisation of the days when I was a child, good manners, efficiency and stability, all fast disappearing elsewhere. It was still a time of austerity despite the war having ended ten years before. Rationing had only just ended, and little at Buckingham Palace had been renewed since Queen Mary's time. It is also home to many people who live and work there in very different capacities, both upstairs and down.

Windsor castle is more beautiful; much, much older and more historic, and is I think the Queen's favourite home. I have been there in several different capacities, both privately for Caroline Lascelles' wedding in St. George's Chapel and the Waterloo Chamber, and for Garter and other services. But best of all was a visit I paid alone some years ago.

It was a chilly February day and an anniversary of the Queen's accession. I was in London, so decided to go to Windsor castle for the day for purely nostalgic reasons. There was nobody there at all except staff, so I was given a private tour and able to wander at will and at length through the beautiful State apartments, including the red and the green drawing-rooms and the Long Gallery with their wonderful pictures and furniture. Some of these have been shown since on excellent television programmes. Unlike some castles these rooms are full of light from the many windows looking out over the Great Park; and they have a delightful lived-in feeling as do all the other Royal homes in which I have painted. Apart from the Great Hall and the Waterloo Chamber the rooms are not vast and high

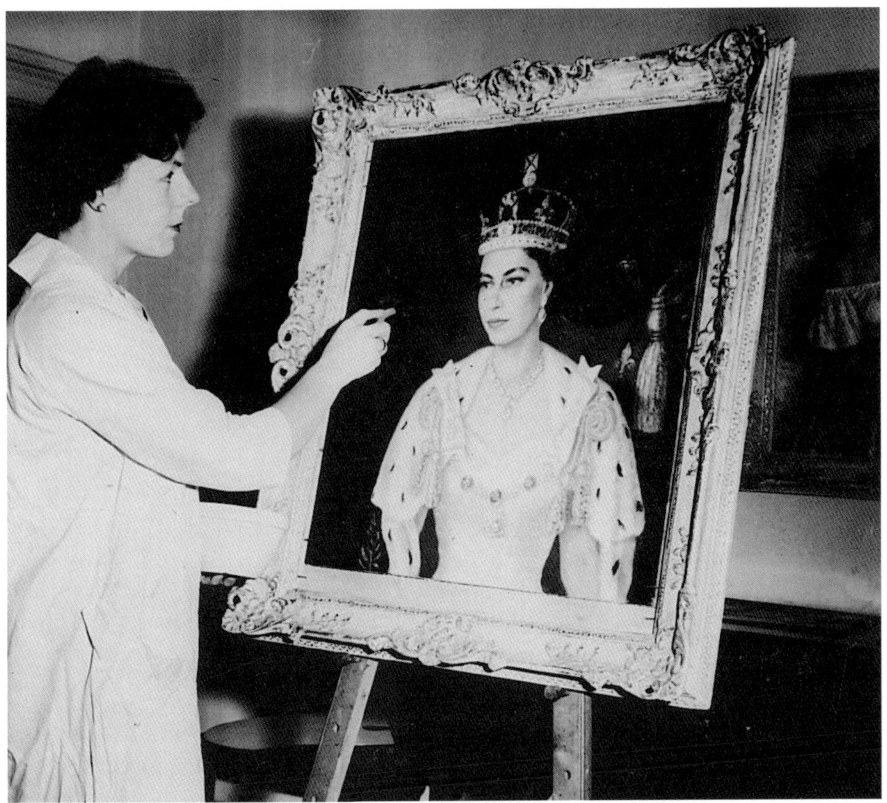

Lydia finishing her second, smaller, painting of The Queen, 1959

(By kind permission of The Central Office of Information, London)

ceilinged as in Buckingham Palace, and of course only part of the Castle is occupied by the Royal Family. There are grace and favour residences, rooms for the staff-in-waiting and other staff, as well as archive and muniment rooms and so much else. Windsor Castle, together with the Tower of London are, I believe, the two places most visited by tourists in England at all times of the year. The Queen entertains all her most important guests and official visitors there.*

It was for me a delightful, happy day. I paid a quick visit to Eton too where I had not been for many years, the scene of so many good parties on the Fourth of June, which is a school holiday to commemorate the birthday of George the Third; a great occasion for boys and old boys, their sisters, parents and older girlfriends to meet for picnics and to watch the cricket. Then, we all forgathered at the Burning Bush, a sort of lamp-post and meeting place from time immemorial, now moved ... the road has been widened; and gone is the great firework display.

In 1974 I was asked to paint several views of Windsor Castle for the Duke of Edinburgh's Royal Regiment ... the Berkshire and Wiltshire, so I came to know it quite well. These watercolours were all done from the park or the river, and I kept a favourite one for myself – a view from the hill looking over the Long Walk with the Castle in the distance from a private part of the park.

How tragic that since I started this chapter much of Windsor Castle has been destroyed by fire. Although the private apartments were not burnt the stench of smoke, charred house, and devastation will remain for months. A burnt house smells like absolutely nothing else ... quite dreadful, as we have come to know too well in Northern Ireland.

A footnote to this fire was a weird premonition I had on the evening of the Prince of Wales' wedding, such a beautiful, happy occasion which like most people I had watched on television. In the evening there was a great firework display in Hyde Park, ending up with a montage of Windsor Castle in lights, with masses of fireworks going off inside; but this gave me a sudden feeling of fear ... of ill-omen. The fireworks ... rockets and so forth ... all looked as if the house was exploding and gave off clouds of lurid smoke. I hoped then it was not an ill omen for the marriage, but never dreamt it would include the Castle too. It was such a chilling feeling that I have never forgotten it.

I painted the then Princess Royal, Princess Mary, in 1956 at St. James' Palace, and found her a charming and delightful model with a great sense of duty. She was quite prepared to stand for all the 'sittings' though already over sixty ... it was a standing pose in uniform, but I was able to manage without that for the most part. She was intensely musical and most interesting to talk to on a wide variety of subjects.

My last royal commission was to paint Princess Margaret. She was Colonel-in-Chief of the Royal Scots Fusiliers, and in 1959 young and beautiful, but said then to be difficult.

A portrait of her had first been mooted two years earlier by Major-General Robert Urquart, Regimental Colonel of the Highland Light Infantry. They already had a portrait of her done some time before, (but wanted a better likeness). This first project fell through no doubt for that reason. Soon after however a portrait was again requested, this time for the Royal Scots Fuseliers. Major General Sir Edmund Bramwell-Devis wrote to ask if I would paint it. I was delighted, and later received the following rather amusing letter of mixed metaphors:

> *"Dear Miss de Burgh,*
>
> *I made a preliminary cast over Clarence House about two months ago and got a somewhat rusty reply.*

The trouble is we are always asking H.R.H. for this and that ... and from considerable experience each has to be dealt with when the wicket is good, so I intend to have another go when I consider the moment is propitious.

As a Regiment we very much want to have a painting of our Colonel-in-Chief ... and I would like to say how much we like the paintings you have already done of the Royal Family ...'

His casting, or bowling, or both, seemed to be meeting with success and the commission assured, when the Ministry of Defence threw a spanner into the works by deciding to amalgamate the Highland Light Infantry with the Scots Fuseliers. Many other regiments were being forced to unite to cut costs, as they are again today, causing tremendous sadness at the loss of identity and historic battle honours. But the two in question suffered from an even worse problem because the H.L.I. wore the kilt and the Scots Fuseliers wore trews ... tartan trousers ... being a lowland regiment; and each had their own tartan. No agreement could be reached on which garments the united regiment should wear, nor on much else beside. Things reached such boiling point that both Generals resigned, and sad to say the portrait project was abandoned with them.

In 1971 however it was mooted once more by a Major General Dunbar who asked me to paint the Princess, but he fared no better. By that time she replied that she would only sit for an unconventional portrait ... abstract, I gathered, which needless to say was not what the regiment wanted. I never discovered the result of the kilt versus trews conflict, but rather think the amalgamated regiment now wears trews in the other one's tartan.

Quite apart from the tribulations of an artist, the sad thing about these continual cuts in the armed forces is that the U.K. is then invariably involved in unforeseen fighting in some equally unforeseen country without the necessary strength to meet the demands.

Fortunately for me the army remained a good customer for many years mostly in a private capacity.

In 1960 I went to stay with friends, Peter and Mairi Lowis. Peter was in the Kings Dragoon Guards and stationed near Hanover in Germany. Being as ever extremely strapped for cash ... I was then still fairly tied up at home looking after my failing parents ... I went by a small Dutch cattle boat from Dublin to Rotterdam which cost forty pounds return. It carried two passengers, a nun and myself, in two comfortable cabins. Alas, the comfort ended as soon as we got out of Dublin Bay. A March gale was blowing and our barque was rolling like a porpoise, with the inevitable result; we were extremely sick.

By the end of the second day, despite useless profferings from the steward, I was more dead than alive. Then there was a knock on the door and in again came the steward bearing what looked like a glass of thick cream, plus an order from the Dutch captain that I was to drink it at once, and that if I was not up on the bridge in one hour he would come and pour it down my throat himself! Faced with such a prospect I closed my eyes and gulped. It was delicious. I took another gulp and sat up; nothing happened; the cabin sopped reeling round me, my head cleared, and within the hour I was up on the bridge being regaled with more of the same!

It was an 'Alexander', a mixture of brandy, cream and curacoa, and unbelievably it had done the trick. The poor nun, I am afraid, could receive no such ministrations and remained unseen.

The voyage took two and a half days, and from Rotterdam I got a third class ticket on a slow train to Hanover which took another day. The train was almost empty and we jolted across the north German plain. It looked very drab and grey in winter and my carriage had only slatted wooden seats, no restaurant car, but we stopped quite often and one could buy kalbschnitzels ... veal cutlets ... and coffee from platform vendors at the stations. I was quite happy and felt I was seeing life. Most of the German I had learnt at school consisted of pious proverbs ... sprichtworten ... and tales of knights on fiery steeds rescuing captive princesses and the like; but it got me to Hanover alright.

Staying with the Lowises was always fun. They had Event horses, so Mairi and I rode a lot in the bitter east wind, often with friendly Germans who lived nearby. Hanover, especially the Ducal palace, was still badly flattened by the war, but Wolfenbüttel where the regiment was stationed, being small and rural was quite untouched, with pretty timber-frame houses and cobbled streets. The army houses were not pretty but they were very snug, except on Sunday mornings when the German boilermen had a day off and did not come to stoke the coke central heating; all the husbands had to cope instead with much cursing and confusion, clouds of smoke, and no heat.

Several of Peter's brother officers asked me to paint their children which was a great help to my finances. One wriggling small boy was simply strapped into his high-chair and left to my mercies. I was still struggling to depict him when Frau Zutt, their old German maid ... she was also ours ... came in and saw the picture.

'Ach, der kleiner Charles!' she exclaimed with delight. I was delighted too ... that it was recognisable.

Frau Zutt was less popular with Mairi and Peter as she got fits of deep depression ... usually if Mairi had forgotten to pay her wages or Peter had left no money for them ... when she broke large quantities of expensive dinner plates. 'Really darling, it would be much cheaper to pay her, wouldn't it,' said Peter sadly.

CHAPTER 13

GERMANY 1987

MY LAST VISIT TO GERMANY was many years later in 1987, long after the deaths of my beloved parents. I had always wanted to visit the famous art galleries in Munich where some of my favourite pictures hang. Young German friends, the Niewrzellas, fans of my rock-singer cousin Chris de Burgh, had asked me to stay with them near Heidenheim afterwards.

This time I did not go by cattle boat as there was not time. I flew out and stayed at a little hotel near the station. It was noon, Monday, when I arrived, and snowing hard, but I set out armed with a large map. The Alte Pinakothek was my goal but all the street names were obscured by snow.

There was no-one much about, but after a brisk walk of three quarters of a mile I found it, huge, dark and firmly bolted and barred. There was no sign that it would ever open again; only a sign in German saying that it was always open. However I way-layed a German lady walking her dachshund (which was literally ventre-à-terre in the snow.) Together we studied the sign and made a complete circuit of the building, to no avail – there was not a chink anywhere. Could it be shut for the winter? She did not think so, very polite and apologetic.

Foiled, I decided to try the Residenz, the palace where the ill- fated last real Empress Elizabeth of Austria had lived as a girl, about half a mile further on. By now I was back in the old city which is a walking precinct, full of fine old buildings of which Müncheners are justly proud. Although many were bombed in the war they have been rebuilt exactly as they were, no modern eyesores. Alas, the Residenz was impregnable too, and when something is shut in Germany it is very shut indeed. There was not even a step one could sit on, and the garden seats all carried six inches of snow. Looking like the abominable snowman myself by now I went into a very smart dress-shop opposite, where a beautiful girl told me the palace was usually open ... perhaps it was closed for lunch? so I retreated to a nearby beerstuben. Here all was warmth and light and people. Everything was pretty, jolly and clean like a country inn. I sank on to a chair, sank my nose into delicious weisses-beer, wiped the steam off my spectacles and ordered the famous dumpling soup. This, sad to say, was not delicious, but hot and nourishing.

By now it had stopped snowing so I set off again. By now too I had realised that few Germans below High -School standard spoke English, and those above it had the sense to stay indoors. The strong Bavarian accent is very hard to understand but by standing in the middle of the road with my map spread out kind people rallied round and it transpired that on Mondays everything is closed, like France and Italy; except the churches.

They looked closed too, but I hurled myself against a huge door. It flew open, and I arrived in the beautiful 11th Century St. Peter's Kirche like a cannonball, bowling over several devout Müncheners en route. This is Munich's oldest parish church with a very impressive interior ... baroque over mediaeval, which I could sit in and enjoy. I could also understand the priest.

Much restored I visited several other churches; and in the middle of the city is the Neue Rathaus, very ornate and gothicky ... it has a famous clock with figures which perform at eleven o'clock. In summer this square is packed with tourists, and I was so glad it was winter. From there I drifted to the market which is well worth seeing especially for the hot-dog stalls ... choose your own sausage from the many different kinds, and hot sliced ham. There were also stalls for every sort of cheese and wine. Greatly mellowed, I did several more churches and some lovely shops. The pastry shops can be smelled from far away and are mouthwatering, with chocolates, bon-bons and every kind of cake. I ate delicious Black Forest gateau full of real cherries and liqueur. Why is it food never smells like this in England? ... perhaps because it is so seldom cooked fresh in the shops. None of this food was expensive, but restaurants were immensely so.

I walked back to the hotel via the ancient Tower Gates of the old city boundary, stopping for various garbled conversations along the way. It was all great fun.

Next day was fine and bright. I found a bus stop; more confusion, it had a machine which shot out tickets upon receiving masses of deutchmarks provided you knew (a) where you were going, and (b) how to work it. It was so new even the locals were baffled. We eventually extracted a ticket for the then vast sum of £2.50, a kleincart, which apparently does several journeys. You get it punched again on the bus by another machine. If you don't get it punched they told me gravely you can go on using it but if caught you are fined £500 or go to prison; so I got it punched.

This time the Alte and Neue Pinakotheks welcomed me with open doors (and charged £3) The pictures were marvellous, beautifully lit and hung, unlike the Florentine galleries. I was especially interested in the fine 19th Century German painters all unknown to me and at that time to the art market, though they have now zoomed into fashion. There was a newly opened room of British Masters, and what should I find there but a fine Lawrence of the Regency Duke of Abercorn, and another badly restored picture of his children. There was also the lovely Romney of Mrs Clements which I had last seen at Ashfield in Co. Cavan when staying with Marcus Clements, who owned it. It is sad to see these portraits no longer where they belonged in Ireland, but good to know they are well cared for. Who, though, will know the people or anything about them?

Munich was of course the chief town of Bavaria, the last Grand Duke being Ludwig who built so many fairytale castles before drowning at an early age. He was the strange, handsome, artistic cousin of the aforementioned Empress Elizabeth of Austria who spent several seasons foxhunting in Co. Meath, which she said were the happiest days in her life.

Next day, snowing and foggy, my young German friends collected me and we drove eighty miles to their modern home, via Ulm and the Blue Danube, which looked very black and cold. They were kindness itself and in the brief forty eight hour visit we went to the marvellous Steiff toy factory nearby where the Teddy Bear, complete with Steiff 'button in the ear', was invented, in 1905 I believe. There were such lovely soft realistic animals there that I fell in love with all of them and bought a little wild boar, partly because it is the crest of my mother's family the Campbells, and partly because it was irresistable; there was a factory shop for seconds. I often worry about the extreme ugliness of children's toys nowadays ... muppets, morph, cabbage patch and Barbie dolls. How can they learn the difference between the beautiful and the merely 'cute'? Perhaps it is all part of the levelling-down process? ... but why not level up?

Next day we went to a large and handsome baroque church near Neeresheim which I wanted to see, complete with monastery; also a story book pink castle with pointed towers surrounded by snowclad trees. This belonged to the Prinz von Thürn und Taxis ... he owned several others ... and was just what I had imagined a real Bavarian castle should look like.

Since then the Prince has died and his beautiful wife, many years younger, who used to flash through Heidenheim on her motorbike with long hair flying, has had to sell some of their houses, and the famous family jewels including the Coronation tiara of Napoleon's Empress Josephine, to pay his debts.

Next day my friends drove me to the airport and in two and a half hours I was back in warm, wet, muddy London, feeling I had been away for weeks, with more lovely things to think about alone on the long winter evenings.

CHAPTER 14

TRAVEL AND VILLAGE LIFE

IT MAY SEEM TO MANY PEOPLE that I have spent most of my life travelling, but in fact while my parents were alive, and old, I could only go abroad about once in three years. This was partly from lack of money but mostly because there was no-one else to look after them.

In 1963 we had moved again, to a new and smaller house which we had built half a mile out of Seaforde, a Georgian type bungalow ... in those days a complete innovation. It was lovely, and my father had helped me to make a beautiful garden there, of one acre, amid surrounding fields.

Both parents lived to be eighty seven, and my mother being four years older, this meant coping with their sad and desperately depressing decline for nearly fourteen years. Although we had excellent daily help for three hours five days in the week, for the other twenty one I was on my own. My parents hated old age, failing memory, hearing, and crippling arthritis, and one knew this could only get worse. Apart from the loneliness the thing I lacked most was any form of human moral support, except from one or two very kind friends.

There is much publicity now about single people caring for aged relations, but then no-one wanted to know about it, and I suspect things have really little changed. Cooking, cleaning, mending, and running messages must go on.

So, short visits to friends in Ireland or London shone like stars. I managed to do some painting and to exhibit in London even when I could not go there myself.

Then in 1969, only days after my mother died, the 'Troubles' broke out here, followed by the oil war, which made life even more circumscribed because prices shot up. Of these days I have already written in 'Lydia's Story'. There were of course compensations ... my beloved Border terrier, the beautiful country, the flowers, and especially books ...

A few years later my father also died, and I suddenly found myself alone and slightly bewildered, with a house of my own for the first time at the age of forty seven! Alas, this had been preceded by two other great personal sorrows, so although I was free it took a while to get myself together.

I did this by working for some old friends the Tenisons, in Jamaica, as assistant manager at their plantation and lovely countryclub, Good Hope. During those five months I was so busy there was little time to grieve, or worry about the house and my future, so this did a great deal to restore my strength and morale.

It also renewed my longing to travel, to discover new and beautiful places and things. The first country I went to was Sri Lanka, and it was quite one of the most lovely; the next was Thailand. By then the East was firmly in my blood.

Many new and interesting people had come to Ulster because of the Troubles which it was becoming clear were not going to end quickly. Some of these became friends, and bought my paintings which was a great help financially. This became my travelling money, my 'exploring' fund!

Meanwhile I resumed more or less normal activities in village and social life, music, the Irish Georgian Society and other creative interests. I loved having people at the house which had been difficult before.

Having been brought up in a Christian family with the standards and values this includes I have been a practising member of the church all my life, despite the horrors of war, and other trials which can shatter peoples' faith. So in between expeditions my life continued in a much more down to earth fashion with long stints of work at home and various public duties ... I was, it seemed, because of my painting and other achievements, still something of a public figure.

Parochial life can be far from dull. In 1976 we needed a new organ for the church at Seaforde and much money had to be raised. Henry Dunleath, being an expert on Organs, found us a fine, small, old one from a church that was being demolished; but we still needed £2,000 to install it.

Patrick Forde who gives unfailing support to this church agreed to have a fête in the grounds of his demesne, and Henry agreed to open it. My contribution was to run a 'Good as New' clothes boutique which was then quite a novel idea, though extremely popular now.

Everyone worked liked Trojans ... there are less than sixty families in this parish, many of them single ... but it was a glorious summer day and the park looked lovely. People came from far and wide and it was an entirely non-denominational occasion.

The only hitch was the opening ceremony. The police band did not arrive because it was busy chasing terrorists after a car-bomb exploded in Castlewellan. So the Fordes, Dunleaths, the rector Mr. Drummond, and Father Brady clambered up onto the old Forde carriage, only to find that the microphone did not work. It emitted nothing but a series of burps and squeaks; so they all had to clamber down again, defeated.

I was doing a roaring trade in my double tent helped by a friend Susanna Mitchell who was 'On the Door' chatting up the queue and keeping it happy while Loraine Jennings and Ita Keenan helped me with the clothes. We were also helped (sic) at intervals by Louise Mitchell aged three and a half who sat on a chair with her eyes sparkling and her short legs sticking straight out chanting 'two more, two more!' while her mother Susanna kept saying 'Louise you must not say two more unless you are sure two people have come out!'

Luckily Emily Forde, Patrick's daughter, took her away and bought her a very small goldfish in a plastic bag of water, which she clutched to her bosom in a state of bliss, while the goldfish had palpitations in a snowstorm of fish-food.

Inside, clothes were whirling in all directions. Our main tent, supplied by the Army, was very smart with real plastic windows, but small, so the men had rigged up an annex which had no light at all where the ladies could undress and try things on. All went well until one old lady's deaf aid got entangled in the mauve woolly dress she was trying on and a vital part fell out, in the dark. This was disastrous as although she could tell us what

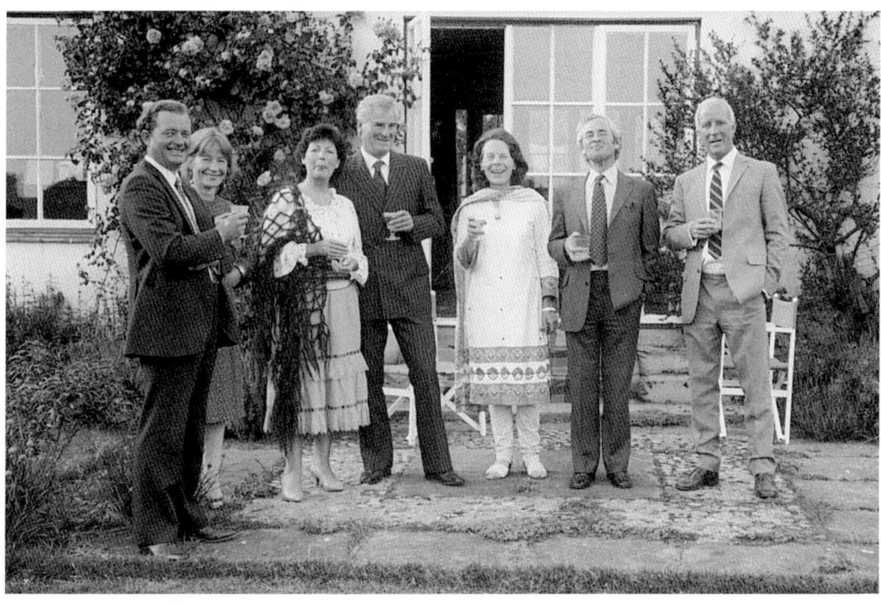

My 60th birthday, 1983, Coolattin.
Patrick and Anthea Forde, Maeve and Roger Hall of Narrow-Water, Myself, Donald Mitchel and Teddy Archdale

was wrong she could no longer hear a word we said. People were despatched for a torch and help, and the next thing I saw was Henry Dunleath standing amid the ladies in the changing room in his bowler hat, while Patrick and a lot of Boy Scouts started to roll up the sides, unaware that the tent was still full of ladies in various stages of undress and alarm.

Henry, who disliked making speeches and had been well doped with lunch by the Fordes, had happened to be passing, and was now saying 'Roll up, roll up, and see the ladies changing!' He then joined Patrick and the scouts who by this time were on all fours quartering the ground like bloodhounds. This kept tremors of consternation passing down the queue but trade continued unabated. Every now and then a friend of the deaf lady appeared before me like Hamlet's ghost and wailed 'They have not found it!' Alas they never did; but my stall made two hundred pounds, and altogether the fête cleared over the two thousand pounds that we so badly needed.

Now in 1996 Seaforde is still a village community ... just, with farmers round about, (and Clough half a mile away is not much bigger), but here we no longer have any shops.

CHAPTER 15

LEGUMISHERA

AFTER MY FIRST VISIT TO KENYA in 1959 when I stayed with friends ... all old Kenya hands ... because I had been ill, I took my first paintings of the marvellous wildlife I had seen on their farms to Rowland Ward, the well known Safari firm and Taxidermists in London to show them to the owner Gerald Best. To my delight and surprise he promptly signed me up for a ten year contract, giving him first refusal of any painting I did of African game. He later gave me much useful advice as well about selling my pictures.

Talking one day about lions he said 'You know, I was such a fool; Joy Adamson brought the manuscript of "Elsa" ... that book of hers, here first and offered it to me, and I turned it down! ... wasn't it awful. I told her nobody could be interested in the story of a lioness'! So, in an indirect way I may have benefitted from 'Elsa' in that he did not want to let me slip through his fingers in case of missing another possible moneyspinner.

I never entirely approved of 'Elsa'. It was a wonderful story about a wonderful animal, but I am basically against any large wild animal, no matter how irresistible, being reared as a pet and not as something to be returned to the wild. Too often it has a most unhappy ending ... usually for the animal. Unless like Elsa it is reared by people who really understand its habitat and customs it will be in constant danger, either from mankind and his inventions, or from other wild animals. All young wildlife is entrancing because it can look so lost and forlorn, foolish and playful, loving and clever. Most of these pets start off as orphans and most of them are so pretty. Even a baby crocodile looks delightfully wicked, but it can snap off your finger soon after it is born. Well fed lions in the wild look almost huggable lying on their backs with paws limp in the air, a smile on their faces and soft fluffy beards.

But one may only look; any untoward familiarity would bring the retribution it deserved. Wild animals are 'people'; they have their dignity, and like people, can be treacherous if one invades their personal space.

Once when I was in Kenya news came of a woman who had reared a charming lion cub till it was nearly grown, then passed it on to other friends who had much more room for it. She did not see it for several months, then went there for lunch one day. The lion was lying quietly, on a long chain attached to a nearby tree, and while everyone was having drinks on the veranda, she went over to talk to her former pet.

The next thing they heard was her voice, quiet and desperate, saying 'Help me! Please help me'. The lion had got her by the throat and by the time they got to her she was dead. A frightening story, but not unusual. Later I was told that the best way to scare a lion in an emergency is to bang a metal tray very loudly. This frightens them enough to drop their prey; anything else only angers them more. (One may not in fact shoot a lion unless it IS killing someone).

Many old Kenya residents, I thought, took awful chances. The Millards lived high on Mount Kilimanjaro on a strip of farmland which John had surveyed and cleared from the bush. There were four other farms there known as the West Kilimanjaro Strip, and nothing else for miles. One belonged to Michael Woods, the Flying Doctor, and his wife Susan; another to the Morrison-Lows, and a third to David Stirling of Long Range Desert Group fame. The climate was delicious, being high above the Athi and Amboseli plains, and the views were incredibly beautiful. I loved to watch the purple shadows from the clouds chasing each other across those tawny plains. Behind was the primeval forest, and above that the snowclad mountain peak.

Wheat and pyrethrum flourished there and so too did cattle. Corinne Millard was an old friend of mine from Kildare and I was staying with them to paint her portrait, and also more wildlife for 'Rowland Ward'. I wanted a nice patch of Papyrus to put into a rhino picture, so asked John where to find one.

'Well' he said, 'There's a good patch at the bottom of that small crater down there', pointing to one of the volcanic plugs which lie around the outskirts of the mountain. 'Corinne will drop you down in the Land Rover.'

She duly dropped me at the outer slope and went off to look at a mob of their cattle further on. Cattle roamed free then in East Africa with only a couple of herdsmen in charge of each mob. I climbed up, and over the lip there was a little path far down into the heart of the crater with thick scrub on either side. It was mid-morning with brilliant sun so it was hot and still. I walked firmly downwards. Suddenly it seemed far too still; I slowed down, nothing was moving, not even a cricket, but I had a nasty feeling I was being watched. By what? Further back I had noticed dry pug marks, a hyena's? Possibly a leopard ... though leopards seldom attack humans. The papyrus was in sight, but something told me not to go on. I turned very slowly and retraced my steps without running, running is an invitation to be chased ... and as I reached the lip of the crater I saw Corinne below speeding towards me in the landrover waving her arm wildly, signing to descend. I fairly rushed down through the thorn scrub, tearing my clothes, and she was so relieved.

'Oh Lydia! are you all right?' she cried! Apparently when she got to the cattle the herd-boy had told her that lions had killed two of them the night before. I am sure these lions were lying up, gorged, in the crater watching me; and so it seemed was she.

One happier lion story concerned a young one I had seen and photographed at Colonel Kerr-Hartley's farm further North. He reared orphan animals and sent them off to zoos in Europe, or released them back into the wild if suitable.

This young lion was later taken down to the Nairobi National Park where there was an excellent animal orphanage, and in due course he was put out into the park to enjoy his freedom. Six nights later he was back, roaring outside the orphanage to be let in again. He had not enjoyed freedom at all. Lions are very territorialy minded and possessive, and the wild lions had clearly been beastly to him! For some days he was left outside, but the roars became too hungry and pathetic; the last time I saw him two years later he was lying on his back on the grass in a huge shady cage, toasting his tummy in a patch of hot sun, the picture of bliss. Freedom held no charms for him. He was a particularly handsome animal with a thick black mane, and he appears in some of my paintings. The manes of wild lions are often thin and ragged from fighting, or charging through the scrub. The great thing about the orphanage was that the animals all looked so glossy and well with plenty of room, in their right climate, and getting the right food. The sound of lions roaring in fact always reminds me of a big bull mooing, and ends with a grunt.

All Europeans on the Kilimanjaro strip flew their own small aeroplanes ... Pipers or Pacers, so I often flew down to Nairobi with John, who was on various committees there. It took about forty minutes by 'plane but eight hours by road, which was mostly cart -track. Wilson Airport was told by 'phone that we were coming; we carried no wireless (and no water), so if we had to come down somewhere in the trackless bush someone would have looked for us ... eventually. John Millard was a very experienced pilot and I was never frightened flying with him. John Morrison-Low was still trying to pass his navigation exams so was not allowed to carry passengers ... very frustrating for his wife who therefore had to do the eight hour drive by car.

Early one morning we were all set to fly to Nairobi when misty clouds started to roll down the mountain.

'Oh dear', I said, 'I suppose we had better take off quickly?' 'No!' said John firmly, 'Never, never take off over cloud. You must be able to land again if anything is wrong'; so that was one risk we never took.

Another was allowing the dogs to walk off a lead any distance from the house. Leopards are very partial to dogs and can seize one in no time, so we could not take them riding either.

Often we went for walks in the evening, which were golden and lovely. Sometimes we met an African who stopped to talk, swapping news about the crops, the weather, and people … just like home. Corinne and John both spoke fluent coastal Swahili and he spoke some Chagga … the local language, as well. The Africans were always very interested in me, 'm'geni' … the stranger, John said, and wanted to know where I had come from and whether I was married. They simply could not understand why I was not. 'Are all the men so poor … do they not have the bride-price?' they would ask, 'She must be very expensive'!

One evening we came on an old and distant hut where the man minding their little coffee plantation lived with his family and livestock. After a long and no doubt interesting conversation we turned to go, and the man made a casual remark, giving the wall of his hut a slight push; whereupon it promptly fell down!

'Why on earth did he do that?' I asked. 'Oh', said John, 'He says it is an extremely not-good house … quite rotten … and he wants permission to cut some hardwood in the forest for a new one'. I was much amused, 'rotten' seemed to be a considerable understatement! Clearly the man did not think it was worth coming to see John about, but … 'as he happened to be passing' … Needless to say he got the permission.

Here one should perhaps mention another great problem in East Africa; 'kuni' … firewood, in other words 'bush', which all Africans need to cook on as there is nothing else in the wild. Paraffin is expensive and dangerous in wood-and-mud huts. So much hard wood has been cut from the virgin forests either legally or illegally that it is now restricted; and the bush is disappearing at an alarming rate too as the native population and their cattle soar in numbers due to modern medicine and veterinary help. The land then becomes a desert, the shallow topsoil blows away, and nothing will grow for wild or domestic animals to eat. Droughts abound; what is the answer? One good recent bit of news is that Tsavo which had become an arid wilderness where everything had died, or left, is now burgeoning green and fertile once more.

I always return from my travels feeling that my mind has been well and truly stretched in new and unexpected ways, even if it has only registered how metal trays can come in handy! Sometimes I look at people in the bus and Underground and wonder that it is part of the same world. Once, I shared a taxi from London airport with an oldish woman whose fearless bleached blue eyes seemed to hold in them the distant plains. I asked her from what outpost she had flown in? She was surprised. 'How did you know?' she asked, amused.

'Ah' I replied 'I can tell by your eyes that they are used to wider, harsher horizons'. 'Well you are perfectly right', she said 'I run a hospital on the North West frontier of India. What do you do?' I told her her that I was mostly a portrait painter.

'Then I can tell you must be a very good one if you notice things like that!' she remarked. An encouraging thought.

CHAPTER 16

SAILING

AFLOAT, ONE WAY OR ANOTHER

MUCH OF MY EARLY CHILDHOOD having been spent in Malta, Nice, St. Jean de Luz and Weymouth where my father's ships were stationed I grew up loving the sea while having a healthy respect for it. All the previous Charles de Burghs had been drowned at sea and my father might well have been the same having served for most of his thirty years in submarines, from the earliest Holland boats in 1906. Luckily he was both a clever and resourceful commander; but despite his distinguished career, plus a Great-Uncle who was an Admiral of the Fleet, sailing had never been one of my favourite occupations. Besides not liking being cold and wet ... especially below the waist, I do not have the sort of hair or skin that comes up looking lovely after a fierce north east gale.

The sea was just a part of our lives. I was born under the sign of Cancer the Crab, and we had to cross at least one sea every time we returned to Ireland on leave. I also love long ocean voyages.

But sailing was a different matter. I knew all the words like sheets, cleats, yards and bollards except what they actually meant. Like the young leadsman swinging the lead when asked by an officer if he knew what he was doing, he replied 'Nossir, but I knows the tune!' From rapt reading of 'Captain Hornblower', 'Midshipman Easy', and other nautical books I could have shouted 'Man the yards'!, 'Luff', 'All hands to the pumps'! and even 'splice the main-brace' by the time I was twelve without having any idea what would actually happen.

When, therefore two friends, Tom and Eve Brooke, asked me to join Colonel Hugh Rose as crew in his yacht 'The Maid of Sava' at Rheims in France on the river, many miles from the sea, it seemed a good way of learning more without loss of life and limb. The 'Maid' was a real yacht with a keel, but she was so small Colonel Hugh could sail her across to France and down most of the rivers and canals to the Mediterranean and

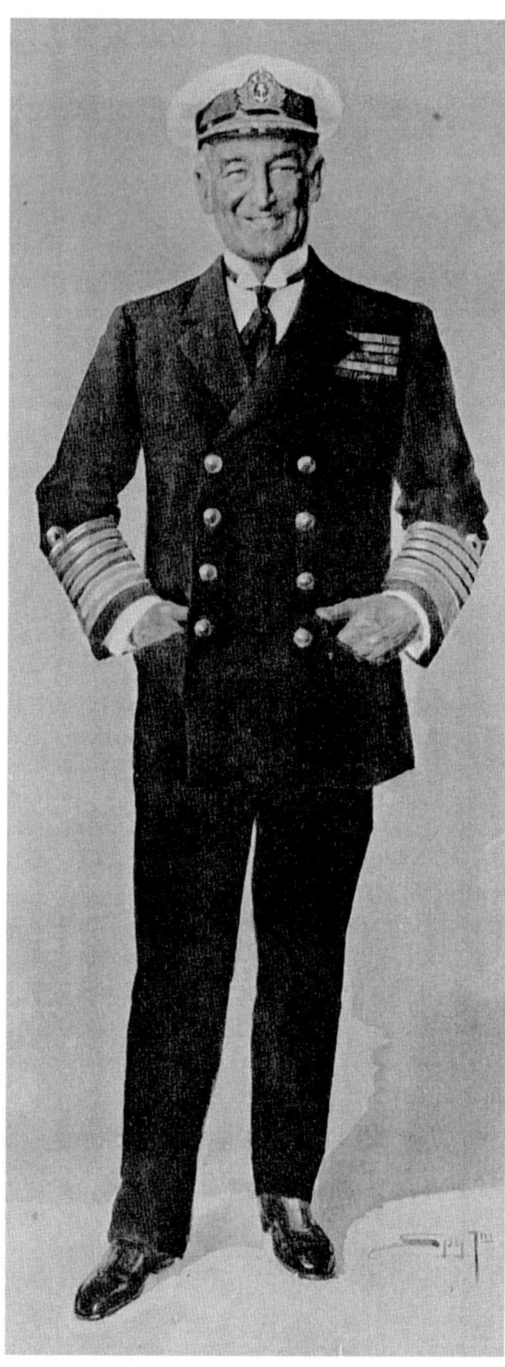

Great-Uncle Jack, Admiral of the Fleet Sir John de Robeck, Bt., K.C.B., D.S.O.

back, which he did most summers. As his wife could not be away from home for so long relief crews joined him at intervals ... some, one gathered, not altogether a 'relief'.

We, the Brookes and I, got off to a bad start. All the French ports were closed because of a strike, so although we were safely aboard a ferry we had no idea where we would land. Needless to say this proved to be Cherbourg, as far away as possible from Rheims, and it was after an awful journey with our bedding and baggage by bus, train, and taxi that we arrived, eight hours late and not knowing whether Colonel Hugh would have waited for us. What joy to find him still alongside, not one whit perturbed. He knew nothing of the strike, but proved to be one of those blessed men who could adapt to any emergency, and he had a delicious casserole all ready simmering on the stove. He was then in his late seventies; his first wife could not bear Army life and had gone off with a brother officer, John Masters, of 'Bhowani Junction' fame, whom she later married. This was hard to understand because Colonel Hugh, whom I had not met before, was one of those special people whom all men, women, children and dogs ... and even French lock-keepers it proved ... automatically love. Very good looking, calm and resourceful, he soon soothed us with enormous drinks.

'The Maid of Sava' was just 23 feet long so with four of us aboard it took a bit of stowing. Colonel Hugh slept in the wheel-house, I had a sort of tunnel along the boat's side with my head up against the sink ... the quarter-berth; and the Brookes slept a mere arm's length away on the table, which wound down till it was level with the seats. So it was all distinctly open-plan; informal was the word. The most unexpected people for instance, turned out to have false teeth; I was wearing my party hair-piece in which I had to sleep as there was nowhere else to keep it except on the draining board. I also had ear-plugs to protect me from snorers, and eye shields to keep out the light; so we must have been quite a spectacle when dossed down for the night. After a delicious dinner we all clambered into bed, the Brookes on the table and me in the tunnel with my head sticking out. Dreamless if not soundless sleep enfolded us.

Next day while Tom and Hugh fettled the boat Eve and I went off to see the famous cathedral. Reduced to a shell in the first war, it had been rebuilt, with new stained glass windows by Chagall, not one of my favourite painters at all but these windows are splendid and glow with rich colour. Soon after we entered a huge procession of singing people burst in from two sides. There seemed to be no way of getting out except by joining them, which we did; they were all singing a lovely chant. Tom arriving later was somewhat surprised to see Eve and me, both staunch Protestants, singing piously from a leaflet, in the middle of the procession.

After lunch we set off by engine power, not sail; we hoped to arrive at Deauville-sur-Mer in a week, in time for the Races followed by a flutter at the casino, so we had each brought one set of party clothes. The river Oise on which we were, is wide but not very deep, so great care had to be taken that we, with a keel, were not washed aground by the big commercial barges which rushed past giving no quarter. At first there was little traffic and we could enjoy the country round about. The routine was to sail from breakfast till lunch, which was always a picnic, snooze till 3 p.m., and sail till we reached an attractive mooring near a village for the night.

In the morning I could not arise until Tom and Eve had got off the table and dressed. Then he and I walked to the village to buy hot croissants and bread while Eve and Hugh cooked the breakfast and stowed all the bedding in my tunnel. I loved those early mornings, with a faint mist rising off the water, and as we walked back through the fields of ripening wheat I sometimes sang the Marseillaise which has such a good tune, so that the others knew we were coming.

While we were sailing there was just space to sit or lie in the sun on deck until we came to a lock, when all was activity. 'The Maid's' ropes had to be made fast to bollards on the bank so that she did not bob about like a cork as the water flowed into the lock, and long sausages called fenders had to be dangled over the side to protect her frail hull. This was my job. Going downstream required even more care with the ropes or she could have ended up dangling like a minnow as the water flowed out. I was banished below during much of this after Tom said sadly, 'I don't know how it is but Ladybird (me) always seems to be standing on the one rope we want to throw'.

The lock-keepers were a great source of news; with barges going up and down all the time news spreads like wildfire. Some grew good vegetables round their cottages which we could buy, succulent peas, beans and courgettes. I took over the cooking and loved the country markets where we would stop to buy food and delicious local wine. We were in fact in Champagne country but drank no Champagne ... it was far too expensive. The country is not really pretty, being wide and flat with high standing crops, but it was all marvellously relaxing; I had been ill and tired, so loved this, and the congenial company.

Some nights on a remote stretch we made a campfire ashore and sat round that after dinner, reciting poetry and travellers tales till darkness fell. Hugh and the Brookes had sailed together often, and all had master-mariners certificates.

One night we were in specially good form after a specially good dinner and several bottles of wine; the bonfire was dying, it was very dark and time for bed. Eve went on board to have first turn in the shower, and switched on the light. We made our own light so had to be sparing with it. 'The Maid' could never get very near the bank because of her keel so we used a long plank to get ashore. Hugh then set off reciting dramatically from Hassan, 'Away! for we are ready to a man, Our camels sniff the evening and are glad ...'

He was just about to set foot on the plank when Eve, below, switched off the light. Profound darkness engulfed us. Then there was an almighty splash ... Colonel Hugh ... and the camels ... had clearly missed the plank!

'Tom,Tom'! I cried, hysterical with laughter but also quite worried, 'Colonel Hugh has fallen in!' Tom was killing the fire but rushed to help. At first we could see and hear nothing but fished wildly. Then there was a gurgle and up came Hugh festooned with waterweed and fairly helpless with laughter. He was a big man, and the bank was very steep so it was quite a job to get him out. Eve, below, was blissfully unaware of the chaos she had caused.

Being August, the French were mostly at the seaside so the river was almost deserted, and the rest of our voyage was uneventful until the last night. The strike was still in full swing so we could not go down to Deauville and had moored at Pontoise, from where the Brookes and I planned to fly home. That last night we decided to have a specially yummy dinner on board with specially yummy wine, to console ourselves for missing the races and casino. This was such a success we were still sitting round the table hours later when my feet suddenly felt cold. I peered down. 'Oh! Oh!' I cried 'The floor seems to be floating!' And so it was. The bottom boards were floating on two inches of water.

Frantically collecting our scattered wits, Colonel Hugh said 'Those new plastic water tanks must have burst!' Earlier we had arranged to fill them with the hose from the municipal swimming pool nearby and this was still running, only now we were no longer filling the tanks but the 'Maid of Sava' as well. Hugh seized the hose and removed it overboard and Tom rushed ashore to turn off the tap. It came away in his hand, and the water flowed steadily on. Tom then went in search of the warden of the swimmingpool. He, it turned out, was in bed with a new wife and had no intention of getting up. Terrified we would be charged enormous sums for the water, Tom, armed with a monkey wrench climbed stealthily up over the fence and after some dubious plumbing directed the water hose back into the pool but still could not turn it off.

The rest of us were baling like mad. Much, much later and fairly exhausted we made ready for bed, hoping the swimming pool would not have overflowed by morning. I had poured out a restoring glass of whiskey for Hugh and another of gin for Tom, also a glass of water for my pills, all in a neat row on the draining board; Eve seldom drank. Hugh reached out a grateful hand and downed the whiskey, then before I could stop him he reached out again and downed not the water but the gin, in one gulp. The hazards of communal living! Needless to say he was not visibly disturbed. Such was my first experiencing of crewing and I greatly enjoyed it. It was just the rest and insulation from the often daunting outside world which at that time I so badly needed.[1]

Of other voyages in cargo boats carrying sugar, bananas, or cattle I have written elsewhere, but some which I most enjoyed were those in the

---

[1] Some years later I painted Angela Rose who was married to Hugh's son Michael, a distinguished soldier. They were an outstandingly good-looking couple and Michael had taken a great fancy to a rather good small genre painting I had done of Miranda Bence-Jones aged 9, in jeans and hugging her teddy bear. He wanted Angela done exactly the same. She had beautiful long slim legs and a curtain of hair but was a poised and elegant creature of forty, not a boneless child. She was hugging their Jack Russell terrier. 'You must slump more' I cried. 'I CAN'T slump' she replied, 'I was always told to sit up straight!'
My efforts to explain the problem to Michael were of no avail. He is attractive and fun, but also an irresistable force, which is probably why he is now such a successful General.
The portrait of Angela turned out rather well especially the Jack-Russell terrier, but alas she has now cut her curtain of hair.

Moghul Steamer. This ancient craft plies, or did, in 1983, from Bombay to Goa and back, carrying deck passengers and cargo. The first class consisted of fourteen cabins and an adjoining dining-room. Below that there were three open decks for passengers, their bundles and bedding, their cooking stoves on which they prepared their food, and that of any livestock they had with them.

The steamer looked to me both old and rusty so that I always feared a good punch in the ribs might go straight through, but we, Kathleen Agnew and I, had a perfectly adequate cabin with fans and a basin, shabby but

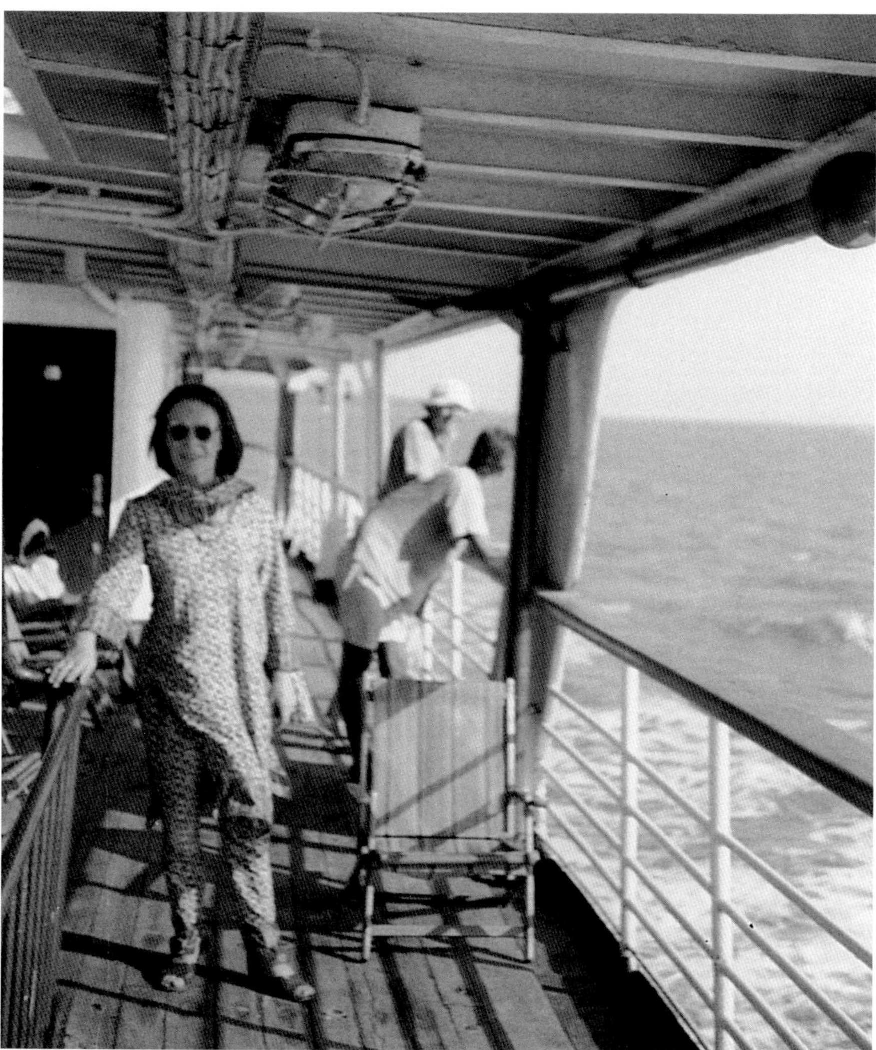

Lydia on board the Moghul Steamer

clean, and very inexpensive. The lavatories were along the deck and pretty awful by British standards; holes in the floor with only a tap; this was not unusual, but in tropical heat it was the smell that bowled one over. However I am a great believer that 'when in Rome do as the Romans do'. I prowled around and behind a door found a large bottle which proved to contain Jeyes Fluid; I pounced on this and sprinkled the contents lavishly around.

The voyage takes twenty four hours, with two stops, and was most enjoyable. After a good curry ... a thali ... lunch, the stewards bundled us out of the diningroom and composed themselves to sleep on the tables, (without removing the table cloths, or taking off their shoes.) We passengers chatted or dozed in deck chairs, basking in the sea breeze. The twelve other passengers were mostly Indian, friendly and delightful. Often we had mutual interests and even acquaintances. Some had worked in Kenya as civil servants before Uhuru ... Independance ... so their pensions enabled them to live quite comfortably in Goa, which still had many British and Portuguese connections.

I loved Goa and fifteen years ago there were few tourists. The Hippies had all been bundled away to a remote beach in the north, but I met one in the street in Panji. He asked me to give him five rupees, about twenty five pence. I was somewhat taken aback; he was a big fair Englishman of about forty, and clearly well educated, but he had one tooth sticking out at right angles through his cheek. I explained that I had no money yet as I was going to the Bank if I could find it. He led me to it and seemed a gentle creature. I fully expected to find him waiting when I came out after the usual awful delay, but no, he had drifted away. I later met him again so gave him five rupees. I thought perhaps he wanted to go to the dentist, but doubt it. His tooth had clearly been like that for a long time.

We stayed in the Taj Village Hotel, then quite small, in the lap of luxury, but I hired a bicycle from one of the waiters and cycled for miles along shady village paths under the palm trees, sketching and taking photographs for my paintings. It was beautiful, and the people and children so friendly and well-mannered.

One morning at dawn I was woken by the sound of something on my roof ... we slept in individual cottages. Upon emerging I found a small wiry little man descending from the palm tree overhead with a large tin bottle. 'Toddy, make toddy' he said, beaming, as I peered into it, and he offered me a drink. I collected my tooth glass, and out of the tin flowed a pale milky fluid with a sprinkling of ants afloat in it. It was delicious! Most refreshing. Every morning after that when I heard him I hurried out with my tooth glass. If one kept the toddy ... fresh palm juice ... till mid-day it became slightly fizzy like champagne. If one kept it longer it went bad.

Cheap and perfectly drinkable rum and brandy is made in Goa, and what I thought perfectly undrinkable wine. They also make fenji from

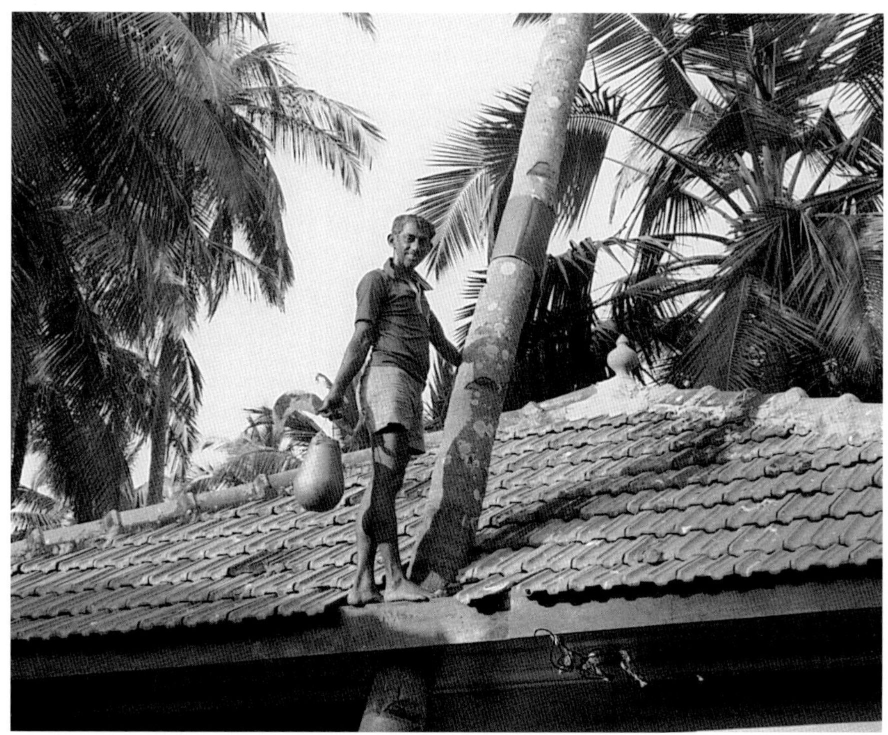

The Toddy Tapper

cashew nuts, which tasted to me indescribably awful like creasote, especially with names like 'Doctors Wind'. Caroline and Johnny Graham of Port wine fame were also staying at the hotel, and we experimented on these together.

On the return voyage of the Moghul steamer they, the Grahams, had acquired the de luxe cabin which we coveted as it had its own loo. Unfortunately it was next the kitchen and they soon discovered it had its own cockroaches too. Primed with this knowledge the next year when I sailed in the same steamer I took a can of insect repellent with me, and at bed time gave a good squirt of this under the bunk and into every nook and cranny. This was a frightful mistake! For the next hour dozens of poor frantic insects of every kind rushed out, including little colourless baby ones that would not have dreamt of molesting us. I fled the cabin feeling like a murderer.

When next heard of the Steamer was ferrying the Indian Army to Sri Lanka to fight the Tamils and try to restore peace, but I hope she is now back on her normal route again and continues to flourish, undiminished.

CHAPTER 17

INDIA

INDIA HAD BEEN TOP OF THE LIST of places I longed to see – and know – ever since reading the novels of B.M. Croker and Maud Diver as a schoolgirl. Both of them were writing before 1900 so I knew the India of those days could no longer exist; but I hoped to find something of it. There had seemed to be so much of beauty and splendour combined with hardship and danger, and it was a land of horses and horsemanship which I loved too.

My uncle Eric de Burgh, had served in India with great distinction for forty years. He joined Hodson's Horse, a famous cavalry regiment, in 1903 and by 1940 was General Sir Eric, and Chief of the General Staff; so I knew

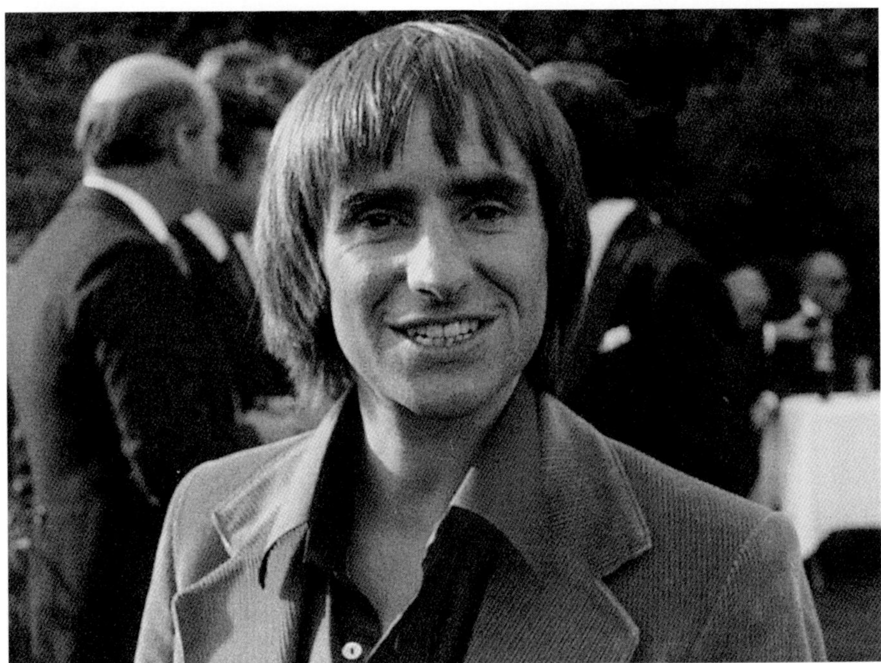

Chris de Burgh, grandson of Sir Eric, at Oldtown

something about 20th Century India too, and had looked forward to staying with him there. Then came the war, in which so many dreams faded. By the time it ended Uncle Eric had retired, and in 1947 India became independent and all the links with it seemed to be ending.

It was not for thirty years that I had the freedom and enough money to go there. Tourism had hardly begun, but I wanted to see Indian life, not just as a tourist, so I wrote to Colonel Walter Shulbrede. He was President of the Hodson's Horse Association, which kept in close touch with the now Indianised regiment, 4th Horse, many members of whom had served under my uncle, who sadly, had died some years before.

Colonel Shulbrede was the greatest help with introductions and advice, but I booked myself into a Cox and King's tour as well for Indian officers are not well paid and I did not want to be an incubus. In case illness befell me I also asked my brother-in -law Robin, chairman of a Bank, if it had any connections in India? He switched me though to their Overseas Department which wrote to the Central Bank of India and the Bank of the Punjab; I could not have been more fortunate.

Our Air India flight was five hours late, and when my group, hitherto unseen, assembled at Delhi Airport – the old one, we met Indian Burocracy head-on. Some busybody official would not let us through after Immigration without a Leader. We explained that our Indian Guide and Leader was meeting us within. 'Oh no', he said, 'You must have a Leader now.' In vain we explained that none of us had ever met or seen each other before; all to no avail. He then pounced on me. 'You must be the Leader' he announced. 'Certainly not.' I said, 'You must ask one of the men!' We were feeling more British and bolshie every minute. 'We don't know each other, and we have not been introduced ; and we do not want a leader!' we chorused. The more he refused the more childish we became. Suddenly he gave in, and we filed through into the arms of our Indian guide, who had been performing a similar pantomime on the other side. We gathered later that the only groups they were used to then in 1977 were Soviet Russians who were always herded like sheep. 'The British invented Bureaucracy', he said sadly, 'and we have perfected it'.

From then on India was pure delight. I had hardly arrived at Claridges Hotel when the telephone rang. It proved to be an Irishman, John Gorman, whom I did not even know except by repute ... he was a distinguished former Major in the Irish Guards; clearly the 'bush-telegraph' had been at work, and indeed this is one of the many similarities with Ireland, everybody is greatly interested in everyone else. I was swept into a whirl of activities, sightseeing with our group by day in the famous Red Fort and Delhi, then enjoyable private parties at night ... parties for lunch too if they could be fitted in. Both the Banks vied with each other in hospitality; the Chairman of the Bank of the Pubjab gave me a delicious lunch at the Bank, and a Mughal picture, but all wore western clothes; while the Central Bank of India took me to the Ashoka Restaurant wearing Indian dress ... achkans, the long buttoned tunic over narrow trousers, which look incredibly elegant on men with even moderately good figures.

I especially wanted to see the President's Bodyguard of Lancers, and if possible to paint them. During British rule they had been the Viceroy's Bodyguard and were splendid horsemen, very like our own Household Cavalry in London; Col. Badhwar of Hodson's Horse, my uncle's Regt. had been the first Indian officer to command it. Dining with the British Defence Adviser I met two charming Indian Generals who quickly arranged for me to go to the stables next day. The wife of the chairman from the Central Bank came with me to translate, lovely and graceful in her flowing sari.

This was just as well, for the taxi driver could not find the stables ... there seemed to be so many entrances behind the Palace. When we finally got there the poor sergeant who had been produced as a model had been stoically stewing in full dress uniform in the midday heat. Colonel Singh was stewing much more abruptly, in his office at being kept waiting. I photographed the Sergeant from every angle, looking noble, but there was no sign of a horse. Would I be hurting his feelings by implying that he alone was not enough? I said 'Ghora?' hopefully, which I knew meant horse in Hindi. It worked like magic, and a magnificent bay horse, fully accoutred, was led out. Unfortunately it too had been waiting and was nearly asleep, with its lower lip hanging down well below its nose. I had grown up with horses until the war and the language of the horse is international, so the grooms and troopers were a great help as I pulled and pushed it into position. The mounted horseman looked spectacular. His dark bearded face beneath the cockaded turban, the scarlet tunic and glittering harness were all I had hoped for.It was the greatest fun!

The Chairman's wife knew nothing about horses, but thanked them all charmingly for me at the end. The photographs proved excellent, and so later, did my painting. The rich colours against the white wall literally glowed out of the canvas, and the picture is now the property of General Sir Richard Trant. I sent photos of it to Colonel Singh for distribution to everyone concerned. Film is very expensive in India, and well beyond the means of the average soldier.

Several of the Cox and Kings group had now become friends, especially Colonel and Mrs. Foster Hart. He had been born in India eighty years before and served there in the police and army until Independence in 1947. His wife, like me, had never been there, and we were both enjoying it so much. He knew the answers to many of my questions about the trees and birds, and what the many words I knew referred to ... like 'chics' and 'kus-kus tatties', which hang in place of doors in the hot weather. A tall, quiet unassuming man, he was, like my uncle, utterly different from the type so

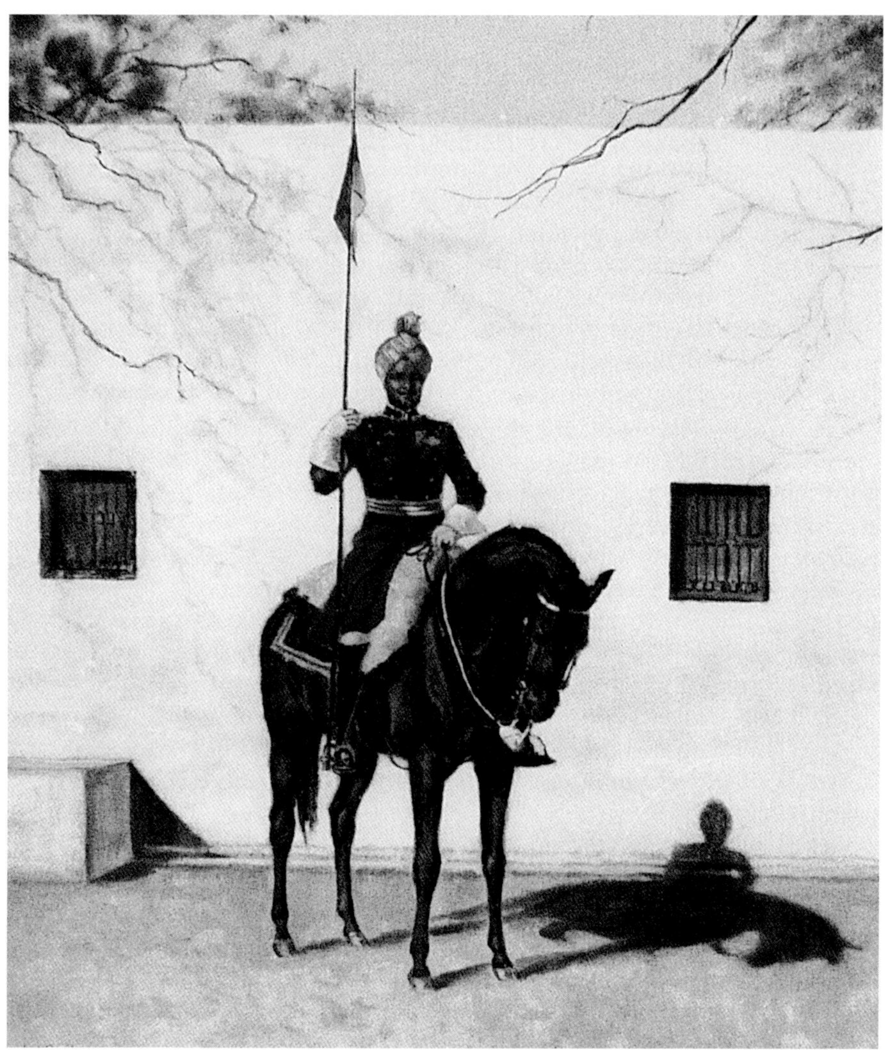

My painting of a Sergeant of the Body Guard, Delhi, 1977

often portrayed on film and television. As we were wandering in the Red Fort I saw a marvellous looking man wearing a brilliant blue tunic, a yellow sash and turban, holding a long seven-ringed bamboo spear.

I longed to photograph him for a painting. Foster said he was an Akhali Sikh, and he was able to make my request in Hindi. I got a marvellous picture of him and he did not seem to mind at all being pushed backwards by me until he was in the right light! This all helped to produce another of my best paintings. He looked such a kindly man with a flowing white beard that it is hard to believe that warriors not unlike him would cause so much trouble in the Golden Temple at Amritsar some years later; which probably led, later still, to the murder of Mrs. Gandhi.

Next day we moved on to Agra, late again, after a very bumpy bus trip with our guide Ali, who was incidentally, the best guide I have ever known. On entering the hotel I was promptly surrounded by people who engulfed me in garlands of marigolds and roses, dozens of them, till I looked like a Hindu deity! Everyone was amazed, but none more so than I. This welcome had been laid on by the local Manager of the Central Bank who had brought his whole family to meet me, and wanted to carry me off there and then. What would I like to do? It was all great fun, but I was exhausted, so we made plans for the next day. Hard on their heels came the Punjab Bank, not bearing garlands but with even more plans; never was there to be a dull moment.

That evening there was Indian dancing in the hotel, and the V.I.P.'s receptionist Mrs. Naby Mithra asked me to join her for a drink first. She was lovely, almost Burmese to look at, and later told me she came from Manipur up near the Burma border. I asked her what it was like there? And she said 'Oh madam, the climate in the valleys is terrible in Summer. The heat and rain are unbearable.'

Though quite young, she was a widow with two children, but of course unable to marry again. Under Hindu custom that would have been disrespectful to her late husband. At least this was better than the ancient custom of sutee, though one Indian lady told me that widows almost might be dead as they were not supposed to go to parties or dance or meet other men. Men often had several wives, so that when they were old the latest wife might well be a girl. Next morning we went to the Taj Mahal.[1] People had told me that it looked just like the photographs; but what no-one had said was that when viewed from without, or the river, it is surrounded on three sides by deep red sandstone battlemented walls, and that the Taj gleams like a lovely pearl above them. One sees it framed in this dark stone machicolated gateway, with the long 'pathway' of water and water lilies leading up to it; far, far more beautiful than I had imagined. That morning in 1977 there was almost no-one else there and the perfect proportions of the domes and garden together with the pearly marble and red sandstone were quite magical. The scale is so perfect that one does not at first realize how enormous it all is. The Taj itself looks over the river Jumna and is flanked on either side by the red sandstone mosques with gilded cupolas and

[1] The Taj Mahal was virtually rescued by Lord Curzon from encroaching jungle, and restored to its full beauty when he was Viceroy, in about 1900, but credit is seldom given for this. Now it is again in very great danger due to pollution from the many factories which have been built in the years since I was there.

wide terraces. The carving on the marble is like the finest lace; every inch of it is carved but so delicately that it never seems too much. The toil of how many hundreds of hands must have gone into making this perfect whole. We had such luck to wander there with only a few Indians in saris about, and some lovely crested hoopoes whose feathers exactly matched the sandstone.

We then visited the much smaller, different, but quite lovely Utmah-ud-Daula, another marble tomb standing by the river, where the custodian's clothes seemed exactly to match the pale cream, white, and browny green of the building. Further upstream is Akhbar's great red sandstone fort with the same battlemented walls and machicolated archways. Here Akhbar had imprisoned his father, Shah Jehan, in a suite of golden-roofed pavilions from which he could look down the river at the Taj Mahal, the tomb he had built for his beloved wife Mumtaz Mahal. It was this view which I had seen in Bamber Gascoigne's excellent book 'The Great Moguls', that really brought me to India. It was so beautiful I could not wait to paint it, and have now done so three times.

That evening the entourage of the Pubjab Bank came to take me for a drive, and asked me what I would like to see? 'Could we find some girls ... women ... drawing water from a well?' I asked. Off we went into the country and soon found a group in a field. They were shy, but intrigued at being photographed with their chattis ... clay water pots. They were slender and graceful too but very poor.

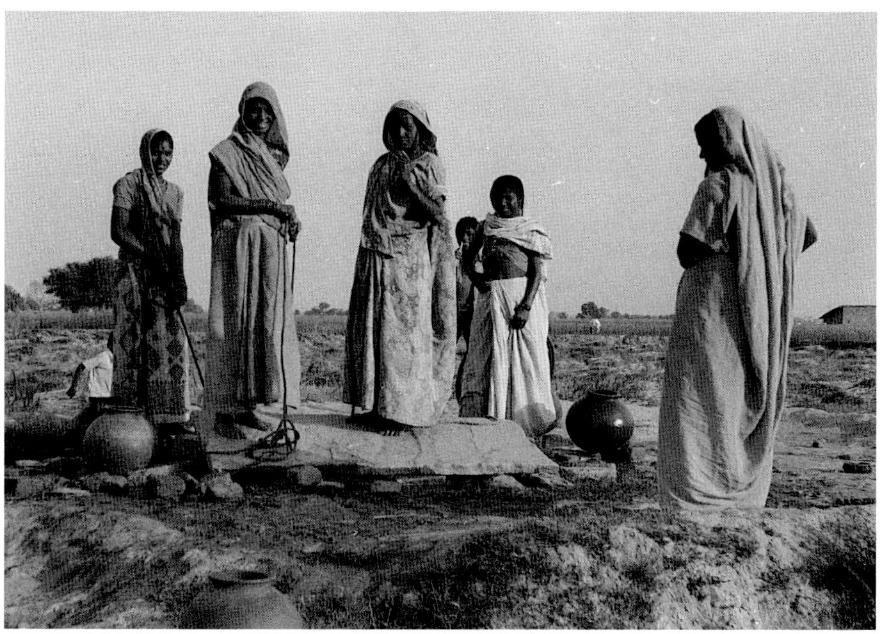

The girls drawing water from a well, near Agra, 1977

They insisted on giving me a drink of water from one of their pots. It would have been very rude to refuse so I drank, and the Punjab Bank had to drink too ... I don't think they had ever done anything like this before! Then we noticed a little man in a grubby white dhoti and turban running towards us. He, it seemed, had a vastly superior source of water at his little hut two fields away. We, girls and all, trooped over there. He dived into his hut and after some fearsome engine cranking, out poured a flood of muddy water from a pipe at the side. He filled a pot with it and I had to drink this too! The little man beamed with delight and dashed off again, reappearing from his garden with a large bunch of carrots! which he washed in the water and presented to me. Quaking somewhat, I duly munched a carrot ... it was delicious, sweet and juicy; (the Bank escort was not so keen to try.) The girls however thought their water was much cleaner ... it was ... so gave the carrots another wash before I departed gratefully with my 'bouquet'. Altogether I could not have enjoyed myself more, and the carrots will appear later in this narrative.

The Central Bank, not to be outdone, produced a magnificent Indian dinner at the manager's house the following night.

While we were there in 1977 elections were taking place amid much excitement, which resulted in Mrs. Gandhi's first fall from power. Many of the Indians I met were glad, including the Maharani of Jaipur, Gayatra Devi, whom she had imprisoned over alleged currency matters, but really for political reasons. Indians are not now allowed to take money or valuables out of India, but the Jais had always had houses in England where they often stayed for polo and racing.

Jaipur City in Rajasthan was the next place we stayed, in the Rambagh Palace, formerly the Maharaja's home and still like a private house, but run as a hotel. It was magnificent and very comfortable.

I loved Jaipur. It was everything I hoped a Rajput Princely state would be. Although Nehru had abolished the Princely States, breaking all agreements and promises, and seized their money, in Jaipur their people still looked on the family as rulers, and very good ones. Polo was still played on the Palace ground and the townspeople flocked out to watch it.

General Anand of Hodson's Horse had arranged a seat for me in the Member's stand and I found myself beside charming Serena Jasbir Singh who became a real friend. Polo itself is not so interesting to me as it always seems to go on at the far side of the field, but the scene was spectacular; ladies in silken saris with long beautifully coiled hair, and men in turbans and uniforms or achkans. There were several Europeans there too, visitors of the Maharani's and the British team which was out to play for the Sudan Cup. Two of them turned out to be friends of my niece's and were good-looking and fun. The Captain was Andrew Parker-Bowles.

Many of the Indian Polo wives wore long tunics over tight trousers, called churidars, in lovely colours which looked extremely attractive on their slender legs. I immediately decided to wear the same, they do look smart on Europeans ... slim ones ... which saris never do. But the polo wives seemed a hard lot. Between chukkas I walked down to the pony lines with Serena who was wearing a deep yellow sari and walked so gracefully. The Maharaja's grooms were all in uniform, with crimson turbans to match

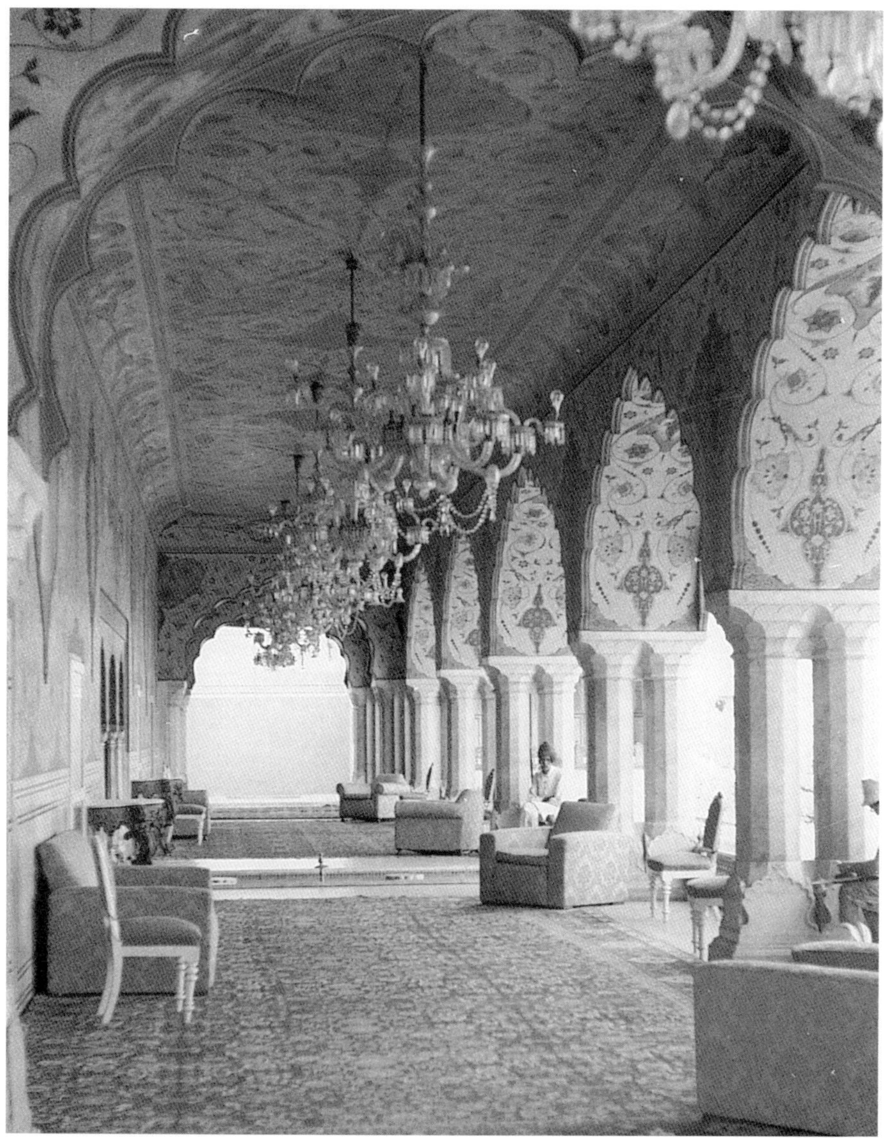

The verandah, the City Palace, Jaipur, 1977

the horse rugs and bandages, and the ponies' coats gleamed like satin. I love the smell of horse and leather. The British team was not doing so well, but they did not of course have their own ponies. Jaipur is one of the few polo grounds still in use in India … the home of polo, where formerly there were hundreds. It is just too expensive, but it is subsidised in a few places I think as a matter of prestige.

That evening there was a great party at the City Palace, now a museum full of beautiful things belonging formerly to the Maharaja … quite lovely, which we had visited that morning; but the Jaipurs still have the upper floor and roof with pavilions on it which, being high up catch the evening breeze and are deliciously cool. There were coloured lights and velvet divans with velvet cushions. The present Maharaja was then a Colonel in the army and known as 'Bubbles' because, being the first son born after daughters, so much champagne was consumed after his arrival. He was charming in what must be a difficult situation; officially he is no longer Maharaja and virtually a guest in his own house. But looking out over the roof tops and listening to the sounds of the night, Jaipur was then still very much an ancient Indian City.

By day too it was a delight. The city walls and many of the buildings are tawny pink … terra cotta really, and every street has its own trade or craft; cloth sellers … where I bought lengths of lovely Rajasthani cotton with Serena; furniture streets, silversmith's streets, grain-selling streets and even a street where men were painting Mughul pictures … all in open fronted shops. In the town centre were camel carts, gharris … horse carts, fruitsellers, wandering musicians, holy men, and even stark naked men daubed all over with ash. People milled around intent upon their business, and a camel would be parked next to a car. There were few Europeans. Both then and during my next visit two years later, I wandered about for hours revelling in the colour and utterly unwestern sights. I felt perfectly safe and no-one bothered me. Later driving out to the ruined city of Amber with my group we passed through some very poor parts of the town where one might not have been so safe.

Jaipur is surrounded by hills and forts, and Amber is one of them. At the foot of it we had to clamber onto elephants. This was purely a tourist gimmick but fun, though not for the elephants who must have been bored to death with it. As usual I was last because I was fascinated by a tiny man in a bright red turban with a tiny sitar, a stringed instrument on which he played a sweet, haunting tune. Mark Bence-Jones, who writes so well about India, had told me of him, and he attached himself to me. As a result I got the last and youngest elephant. I sat on one side of the howdah and a very fat heavy man sat on the other, which made it all lopsided and my feet were in the air. The poor elephant hated it and kept walking sideways like a crab, to the great annoyance of its mahout, who was sitting behind its ears and kept prodding it with a goad. I felt so sorry for it that when we got to the

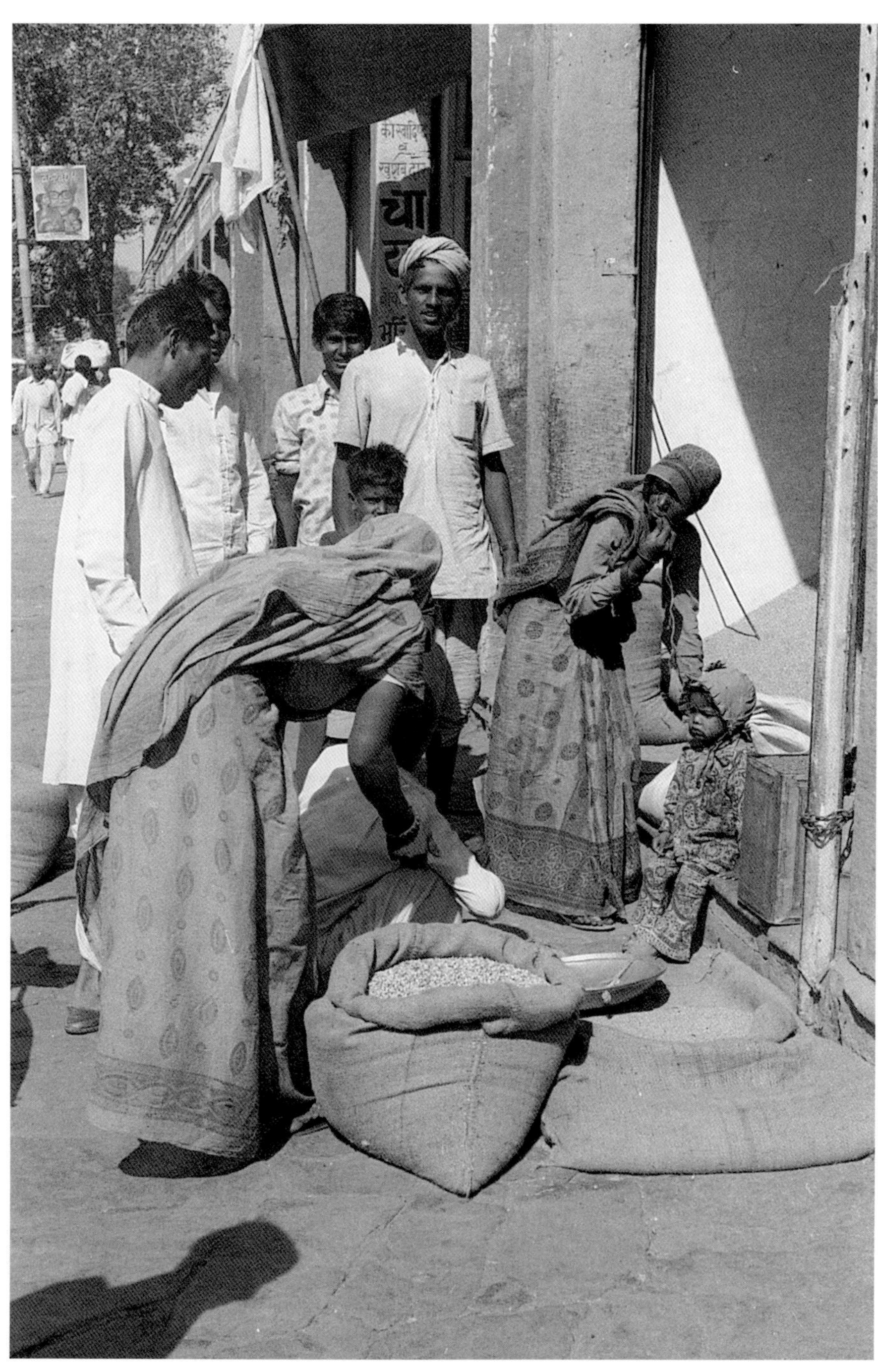

Street scene, Jaipur, 1977. The colours were wonderful

top I fished in my large bag and produced one of 'the' carrots. Its poor face lit up with surprise and it took the carrot very politely in the tip of its trunk; the mahout was not pleased because he thought it had behaved badly, but he let it eat the carrot.

The morning after the polo dance I was exhausted. It was very hot and I was lying on my bed in a skimpy nightdress when the door opened and in came the waiter with the early morning tea. In behind him came two strange men and assorted women. Help! I was looking frightful, and aghast. They proved to be the manager of the Punjab Bank and his family bent on taking me out at once. This I could not do as Ali, our guide, had made other arrangements, though by this time my group were all used to me appearing and disappearing like the grin on the Cheshire Cat. The manager seemed very put out, but I suggested going to them for dinner in the evening.

We sat on his roof in the moonlight and made stilted conversation; I think he was still offended about lunch, but he had his revenge. He produced the MOST frightful drink, which he assured me was much beloved by the ladies. It was made of black carrot juice which was left for two days under the sun and three nights under the moon to ferment, and it tasted perfectly awful. It was supposed, I think, to be an aphrodisiac, but had definitely had too much sun ... or something! I do not remember much else about the evening but they all wore dreary western clothes, the girls too plump in jeans.

Next day we flew to Udaipur, perhaps the most enchanting place of all. Here the Maharana's palace, in part of which he still lives, looks out on the great lake ... man-made some hundreds of years ago. On an Island in the lake is the Lake palace, now a hotel, its marble walls and cupolas glimmering in the waters of the lake, unbelievably beautiful. Here most of our party were staying in sumptuous Mughal suites overlooking the water, complete with tasselled Mughal swings with little tinkling bells, on which one might swing to catch the breeze. Due to a shortage of rooms and being single I was put in a guest wing of the Maharana's palace which was much more decrepit. Our Queen, Prince Phillip, and their entourage had stayed there sixteen years before, but it seemed little had been done to it since, and in that climate rot, predators and mildew soon take over. It did however have a marvellous view of the Lake Palace which looked magical at dawn, at dusk, and in the moonlight. The shutters of my turret room were closed and I rushed to open them. My little bearer ... room servant ... rushed after me and closed them at once, gabbling wildly in Hindi or something. He took me to a window in the gallery looking back to my abode and pointed. There, above and below my widow were the most enormous wild bees' nests I have ever seen. Thereafter I kept the window firmly shut! The door, he indicated, must be kept shut as well. I later discovered that both monkeys, which are sacred because of Hunyamun the monkey God, and pigeons wandered in and out at will and were anything but house-trained. I had an antiquated bathroom, and an enormous reception room with chandeliers, all swathed in dust sheets, and I suspect not dusted either since the Queen was there, for there were monkey-turds and bat droppings everywhere.

It was however the India I had come to see, and the India of 'The Rains Came'. The views from all the other windows ... no glass of course in the hot climate ... was unique.

That afternoon the black carrot juice had its revenge. While sitting on the gilded swing in the Hart's suite at the Lake Palace where we all ate, I suddenly knew I was going to faint, or worse. I staggered down to the boats and waved towards the shore. By the time we got there I had practically passed out and was strong-armed up to my tower by the boatmen and my bearer, hoping they did not think I was drunk or drugged. Once there I was violently sick and passed out completely. Hours later, about 11.30 pm there was loud hammering on my door, and in came a representative of the Central Bank, bearing grapes and khoa ... a fudge-like sweetmeat and delicious at any other time. He was quite undismayed by my disordered state and all set to make plans, but his English was not too good. Groaning and giddy I suggested the following evening.

He and my bearer kept reappearing next day to make sure I was still alive, until furious at missing all the wonderful sightseeing, I clawed myself together and set off for the Lake Palace at tea time. Mr. Sushil Kumar Singhvi, as he turned out to be, had promised to take me in a boat to see the Jag Mandir, Shah Jehan's island with a small ruined palace on it. The Harts came too, and it was magical; the sky was all rosy from the setting sun, and reflected in the lake as we rowed along. So was the island, used occasionally for functions. We wandered in its dreamy desolation of marble pavilions, the wide courtyards guarded by stone elephants, and a deserted garden. Overhead huge bats ... flying foxes ... swooped and soared. To me it seemed pure Omar Khayam: 'They say the lion and the lizard keep the courts where Jamshid gloried and drank deep'. The Harts were delightful companions and with his knowledge of Hindi we were all able to talk together quite well. I also learnt one more phrase ... 'mein baihosh hone wali hoon', which I think means 'I am going to faint', and 'mein thuk gayee hoon' ... I am very tired! Very useful they became as I am often 'baihoshed'. (The black carrot juice is I believe call 'gajar khanji, and to be avoided at all costs!')

Our tour ended in Bombay, not at first sight an appealing place, but on subsequent visits I grew fond of it. On this occasion Rattan Pochkhanawala of the Central Bank and his wife Pilloo took me under their wing, and also asked several of us to lunch at their spacious house in Pochkhanawala Rd.

We enjoyed so much seeing a real Indian home ... the only one the others had seen; Pilloo is a distinguished modern sculptress.

That night the Pochkhanawalas took me to dine with some attractive young relations at the Taj Mahal hotel by the great Gateway to India. This was a most elegant party in full evening dress, and at the end of dinner the ladies were each given an orchid on a plate. 'Are they not going to give you anything?' I asked Rattan sympathetically. 'I think they are just going to give me the bill!' he said wryly.

Upon coming out at midnight I noticed a tired cab horse, still waiting so patiently by the entrance. I stopped, and groped wildly in my bag. Lo and behold there was just one carrot left, and the poor horse was so pleased to get it. Rattan was greatly amused, 'Good God, Lydia', he exclaimed, 'Where on earth did you get that carrot!'

Let it not be thought for a moment that the dreadful paradox in India passed unnoticed by me. It did not; and although I knew much about it before, it is hard to come to terms with. Normally Tourists are kept well away from the squalor and awful poverty, but many of my friends were Indian and they drove by the shortest route, sometimes through slums beyond belief ... that anything could survive in such misery. I will not harrow the reader with details except to say that one must not go to India ... and not only India, unprepared for it. What can one do to help? Very little, I am afraid. Some of the money one spends may filter down to the poor, one hopes, but the country is very poor and the population so vast. British rulers struggled for years to alleviate conditions. It does seem that things are improving somewhat now, but with lower mortality the population just keeps on rising. One cannot fail to be impressed by the fortitude of the people; or is simply resignation?

On a later visit to the Obornes, British friends, I was squirming as usual at the sight of a lame horse with a dreadfully swollen knee trying to pull a cart full of people. 'You have to remember, Lydia', said Margaret, trying to comfort me, 'these people themselves have to work till they drop or they will die, so they expect their animals to do likewise'.

But I do not want to end this chapter on a sad note. India will always be special for me, and I have returned to it three times more, so will write of it again. The two Banks, so different in style but equally hospitable, together with the kindness of Hodson's (4th) Horse, had given me a much wider, unusual dimension to that visit. I felt quite at home, and had no qualms when travelling there alone, or more often with friends.

CHAPTER 18

SOUTH AFRICA

AFTER FOURTEEN GOVERNESSES and two years at the Church School in Durham my parents packed Coralie and me off to a small select boarding school for girls in Suffolk, hoping that we might acquire polish and a wider spectrum of friends. We arrived there in Sept. 1938 just in time for the Munich crisis. My father was promptly recalled to the Royal Navy, and as the school was right on the East coast at Aldeburgh my mother waited there with the car in case war was declared or the Army appropriated our school and we had to be taken home. Then Mr. Chamberlain returned with his brief reprieve, and life at school reverted to normal, though we as a family had few illusions. War did break out a year later, and of the wider spectrum of new friends some alas, were killed, others scattered, and more married almost at once.

My greatest and only lasting friend was Mary Stanley from South Africa whose father was Governor of Southern Rhodesia. Her mother was a Cloëte of the famous Cape Dutch family which was one of the first to settle and farm the beautiful country at Constantia and later near Somerset West.

Of all this at fifteen I knew nothing, but had been greatly looking forward to visiting Mary in S. Africa the following year.

It was not to be. Mary when nineteen married Donald Graham in 1942,[1] in England … I was their bridesmaid … and both her brothers were also in the army, so with all the post-war problems, acute shortage of money, and my illness after the Enigma code-breaking job (manning the bombes) in the WRNS at Bletchley, it was forty years later, 1980, before I finally got to South Africa.

By this time the Grahams had a large and beautiful grown-up family and we were middle-aged, but our friendship resumed almost where it had left off all those years before. This is the marvellous thing about one's childhood friends; all the motley years in between seem to vanish when we meet again.

---

[1] See " Lydia's Story"

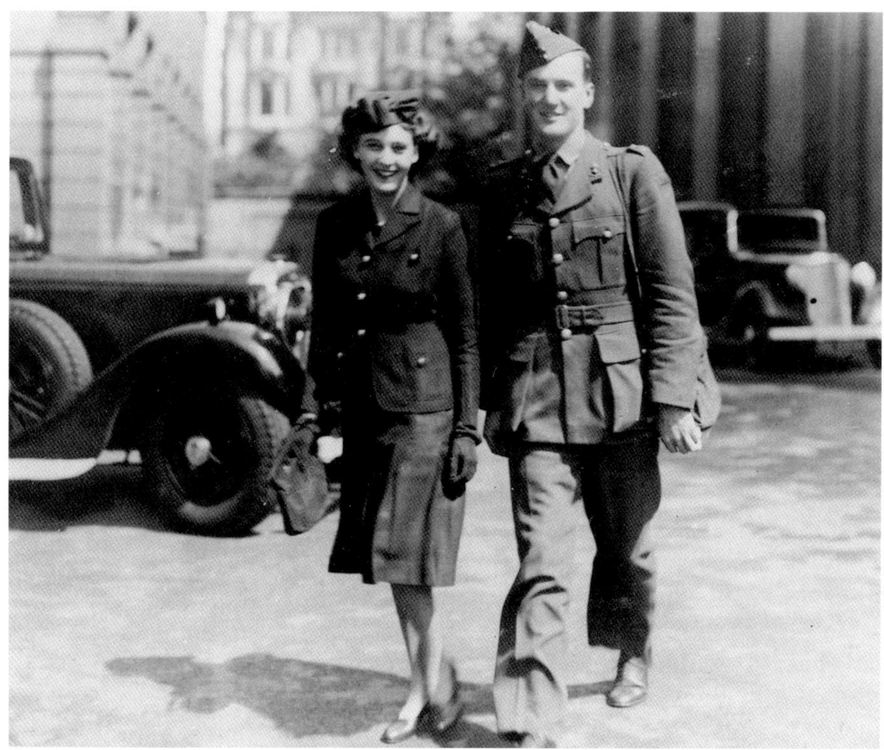

Mary Stanley and Donald Graham, just engaged, 1942, the Guards' Chapel

I loved South Africa. It must be one of the most beautiful countries in the world, varying from the tropical North to the Mediterranean climate of the South.

This was to be the first of many visits. In 1980 Apartheid was still in force. The Afrikaner (Dutch Boer) Mr. Malan had become Prime Minister in 1948, Apartheid was introduced soon after and rigidly enforced. All the coloured population – Malay, Indian and mixed-race people were deprived of the vote, despite many of them being prosperous, well educated and talented. Most, but not all, native Africans had never had it. Many were moved forcibly from their homes to new, restricted areas, and South Africa left the Commonwealth a few years later. Of this and other political ramifications there I do not propose to write. It has a long and bloody history from which no nation emerges with much credit. Even before white men arrived warring tribal Africans were slaughtering each other in thousands, as alas, in Ruanda they still are today. The arrival of white races added to the struggle. Anyone interested in the development of S. Africa can do no better than read James Mitchener's excellent book 'The Covenant'.

Few if any of the Graham's or my friends approved of apartheid and many including Mary worked tirelessly for the Black Sash Movement which started as a protest movement by women against the removal of coloured people from the common voter's roll, and continued to fight for justice and human rights. They also formed advice offices to help, mainly Africans, achieve the few rights that were left to them.

This however is not the Africa that I, as an artist and painter, want to record here. With all their children married and away Donald and Mary had built themselves a very comfortable bungalow at Newlands, a lovely residential area behind Table Mountain between Cape Town and Constantia, with only a tiny garden to maintain; even here we waged a constant warfare on moles and snails! Every morning I awoke to the wonderful view from my bed of the great blue mountain towering above their hedge of bright pink and crimson bougainvilleas, bathed in sunshine.

There are flowers and trees everywhere; literally miles of Watsonias and blue Agapanthus planted along the excellent roads in the residential areas. Everything seems immaculately kept, and so clean, even the water is cleaned. Although quite a number of our friends' parents still lived then in beautiful colonial Dutch houses with lovely gardens and elderly resident African servants who had been with them for years, few but the very rich of our age now had more than a 'daily' three times a week, who had to live right away in the allotted area with few such facilities, and who had to travel in to work. We had Glady, an enormous and handsome Xhosa lady, and Victor who cut the grass and gardened once a fortnight.

The middle slopes of Table Mountain are thickly planted with pine forests where all can walk (but not alone) and have braais and picnics. Huge oak trees give shade along the roads and avenues lower down. All of these were imported originally, and flourish in the Mediterranean climate. A few miles from Newlands is the great Botanical garden, Kirstenbosch. Only indigenous trees and flowers are grown there but these are legion in number and variety, and incredibly beautiful. Of Proteas alone ... the National emblem ... there are hundreds of species with their enormous flowers or vivid hued leaves. Kirstenbosch stretches for miles and we often wandered there in the evenings, always finding something new to see in flower with the forest and mountain as a magnificent background.

On other evenings we went to plays and concerts at the Baxter at Cape Town University, and the City Hall, or to opera and ballet at the Nico Malan Opera House. There was no nationality or colour bar in the arts and many of the performers were of mixed race. I thought the standard of the productions was quite excellent, especially for a community cut off for so long by sanctions and Equity from Europe and the U.S.A., and working on a very small budget. Of course many outstanding musicians from abroad ignored the ban and did come to perform there.

The Graham's great interest has always been music. Donald is an expert musical engineer, so, when he retired he started a recording studio. This, G.S.E. Claremont Records, records much ethnic and other music performed and composed in South Africa, from marimba to classical works. These tapes and discs are obtainable now all over the world. Later, having had a heart attack in the middle of a recording session, Donald moved much of his equipment into his own house and made his studio there, while Peter Kramer continued the business in Claremont.

I always have a feast of music staying with them and have met many of those involved in making it. The most wonderful and moving performance of all was 'Camille', the ballet of 'La Traviata' danced to the music of the opera in the lovely outdoor arena at Oude Libertas near Stellenbosch. This is a great Winery where a sort of small Glyndebourne has been created, and where one can picnic in the gardens, before watching the performance under the stars as one does at Verona. The dancing and choreography were superb.

The Vineyards with their beautiful old Cape-Dutch houses are another great attraction of South Africa ... for me at least, not to mention their delicious wines. The first vines were planted near Constantia which is famous for its grapes and still makes wine, though much of the lovely surrounding farmland there is now an expensive residential area.

Groot Constantia, the Great house, was burnt to a shell in 1925 but later rebuilt just as it had been. Much of the money and Cape-Dutch furniture for this was given by Alfred de Pass, the grandfather of my great friends from childhood days Alfred and Robert. Their father Dan de Pass was in the Navy with my father. The de Passes were Jewish and in the leather business in East Anglia. One son, Aaron, emigrated to South Africa and had begun trading from there by 1849, starting in the west from Walvis Bay and Angra Pequena, now Luderitz. Even having made treaties with the Hottentot King the journeys and distances they must have covered, not to mention problems with wild animals and drought, are remarkable. They owned much of the slipways and shipping rights in Cape Town and Durban during the 19th century, and until 1952 were great sugar, fishing and guano brokers,(not to mention the odd spot of brandy and gunpowder), as well as patrons of the fine arts. Sad to say because Dan, the only surviving son of this empire married Jean Fleming and became a Christian his father cut him off from his whole inheritance, and never forgave him. Groot Constantia however, with its wineries, is a much visited museum today, and there is a de Pass Gallery in the National Gallery in Capetown, as well as that in Truro, Cornwall.

Another lovely house in that area is Alphen which still belongs to the Cloëtes but is now a hotel ... it had been the home of Mary Graham's aunt Nicolette Bairnsfather, a great beauty; and there is a little memorial with plaques to Mary's parents and maternal grandmother there too. Of the many other lovely houses those I actually know are at the foot of the Helderberg mountains between Somerset West and Stellenbosch.

Vergelegen, famous for its huge ancient camphor trees as well as its beauty was built originally by Adriaan van der Stel, but altered considerably by the Phillips in the 1920s; Sir Lionel Phillips was a Rand millionaire and very rich. It is said that Lady Phillips changed her mind so often during this building that she drove the architect mad and he finally shot, not Lady P., but himself. At least he left a beautiful testimonial to his skill. Having changed hands since, it is now owned by Anglo American Farms and has been refurbished for VIP guests and conferences. Delicious wine is being made again in its vineyards. It is open to the public and has a charming restaurant.

Very close to it is Morgenster, even more beautiful, with its great thatched roofs and white Dutch gables and outbuildings,...wineries, manager's house, and stables. Formerly the home of the Van der Byls, it was later bought by Dinkie Cullinan of the great diamond family, married to Leonard Hawkins, which gives Morgenster added interest for me because I painted the famous Cullinan diamond in my second portrait of the Queen. In this she is wearing the Imperial State Crown with the diamond ... presented to King Edward VII ... in the centre below the Black Prince's ruby. Both these homesteads have most beautiful trees and gardens as well as the farms and vineyards, and at Morgenster Shirley Cloëte, Dinkie's (married) daughter, makes beautiful ornamental glassware as well. Unravelling the ramifications of these old Cape families is almost worse than our Irish ones! so I will attempt no more.

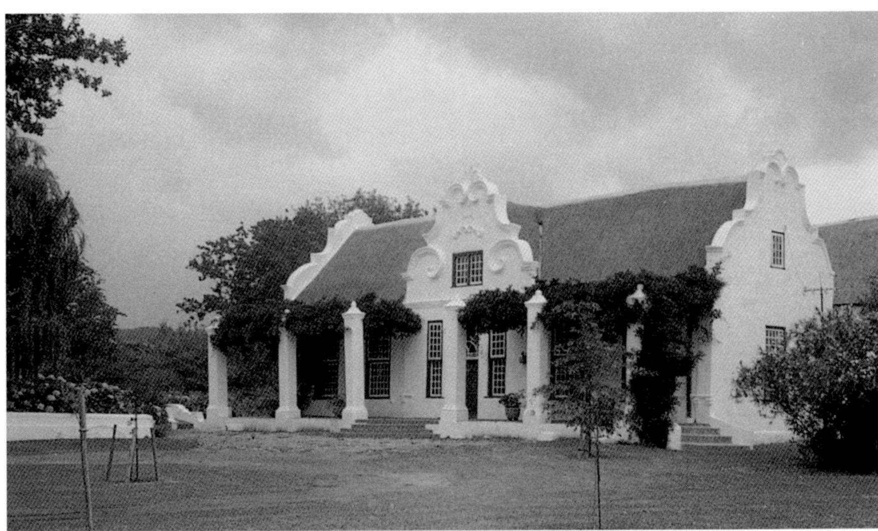

Morgenster, Somerset West, South Africa, 1980

Morgenster has just been sold to Italians because the Cloëtes can no longer manage it, the fate of too many of the old Cape homesteads which were so comfortable to live in. While staying with the Synnotts we went to Shirley Cloëte's farewell dinner party there on the lawn under the full moon.

David Synnott is the son of Pierce who was not only an old family friend and neighbour of the de Burghs in Kildare, but it was in the attic of his house in Thurloe Square that Coralie and I lived while we were studying painting and music in London just after the war; and where we had so much fun[2].

David's mother was a daughter of Sir Abe Bailey one of the younger of the men who developed the goldfields of the Transvaal, and thus also a Rand millionaire. She had returned to South Africa at the end of the war and the marriage broke up. After her death David decided to sell Furness, their lovely house in Kildare, due to family and other problems, and move with Sue to South Africa. There he bought Land en Zeezicht, another beautiful Cape Dutch house near Morgenster and Vergelegen, taking much of his furniture, pictures and library with him. It no longer had vineyards, and the park and garden had been planted up with young Yellowood trees which one is not allowed to cut and are very slow growing.

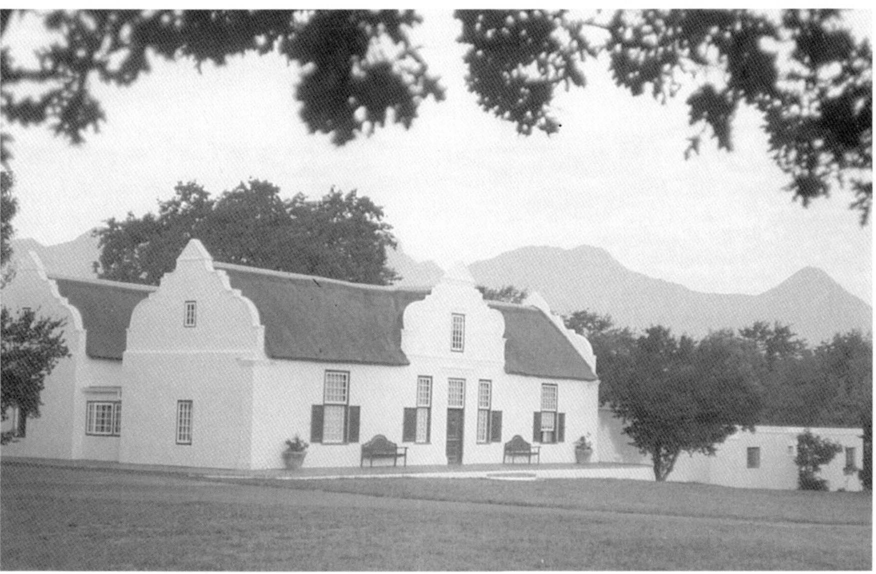

Land en Zeeicht homestead

---

2 See " Lydia's Story"

The house needed much repair and conservation. The roofs of Dutch houses are all of deep thick thatch, and the polished floors and panelling inside are of fine woods, so that in that land of very dry summers bushfires are a constant hazard ... spectacular to watch but very dangerous to houses ... as strong winds can carry the sparks for miles.

Nearby the Horwoods live in a smaller but lovely similar house and grow marvellous roses. Bill Horwood told me his father was in Abe Bailey's cricket eleven when he, Abe, then still a young man, hosted the English team coming out to play for the first time. Alas, when they arrived Abe Bailey and most of his team were languishing in prison for being involved in the Jameson Raid! Fortunately they did not languish for long and cricket was played. Sir Abe later became a well-known figure on the Turf in England as well, and left his fine collection of sporting pictures to the Cape Town Museum, while David has lent some of his to Vergelegen. Perhaps I am writing too much about Cape Dutch architecture; I love it because it is both beautiful and unique. Not only big houses but cottages and whole villages like Tulbagh and Graaff Reinet have the same thick thatched roofs, snowy white walls and high fluted gables. The old town of Stellenbosch is perfectly preserved with shady streets and avenues of ancient trees. In the museums, and the University there is some of the finest sculpture I have ever seen, the small magical bronzes of Anton Van Wouw. He came from Holland in the mid-19th century and stayed to capture so well the spirit of S. Africa at that time, from Bushmen to gold miners. 'The Accused' depicts exactly the uncomprehending acceptance and hopelessness in the young African's pose, while 'Bad News' shows two Boers in the war clearly reading of a death or defeat.[3]

For an inordinate length of time in that war it seemed to be the British who were being defeated while Ladysmith and Mafeking were besieged for many months. Two of my Uncles, and one Grandfather, having fought in South Africa, I had often heard about it. As a girl I had loved 'The Dop Doctor' by Frank Danby, (who was I believe a woman?) a wildly romantic and emotional novel about the Mafeking seige and hardships.

In fact Lady S... W..., daughter of an Engish Duke, achieved considerable publicity not to say notoriety there. Major W... her husband who was in the garrison at Mafeking had expressly forbidden her to come up there when war was imminent. Needless to say she took no notice whatever and arrived driving her horse and buggy, complete with lady's maid. She had arranged to be a war correspondent, she said.

As the siege began at once there was not much they could do about her! However the situation began to pall as communications ceased and food

---

[3] Many of these were endowed by one of the great wineries.

grew scarce, so she decided to drive out again, as she had come, despite being surrounded by Boers.

The next thing the beleaguered garrison heard was that she had been taken prisoner, maid, buggy and all. The Boers sent a message to say they would 'trade' her for some of their people imprisoned in Mafeking. The Commanding Officer[4] refused categorically to trade; possibly not from lack of chivalry. He may have felt the prisoners were less of a problem. It seems the Boers also found her a problem because after quite a while she was seen re-approaching Mafeking in the same way that she had first come!

Her husband alas was killed in action in 1914. It is said that in later life she used to claim that she had slept with a Peer for every letter of the alphabet.

'But what did you do about Y and Z?' asked somebody.

'Yarborough and Zetland, you fool' she replied.

'Yes, well, but what about X?'

'Ah, he was the unknown quantity of course!' Whether all this was before, during or after Mafeking ... or all three, history does not relate!

---

4 Later Lord Baden-Powell.

CHAPTER 19

SOUTH AFRICA

PART TWO

MAFEKING LIES AWAY NORTH to the West of Johannesburg. So far I have never been there, but I did make an expedition on my own to the Drakensberg Mountains ... the Sani Pass, at the South end of this marvellous range. I flew to Durban, got a taxi to Pietermaritzburg and a Greyhound bus from there. This took me by much well-known Boer war territory; Colenso where Winston Churchill was captured, and Ladysmith which was also besieged, though not for so long.

From there one's route climbs into the great mountain ranges which are beautiful beyond belief. The Sani Pass Hotel where I stayed is completely surrounded by mountains, a river and a rolling landscape of tawny Zulu grass which is almost thigh-high. If one walked even a little way amongst this out of sight of the hotel one could just imagine the great Zulu Impis charging up out of the drift. It was spectacular country for painting which was why I went there. There were also spectacular thunderstorms of the sort only Africa seems to produce. Sad to say there is little of the bigger wildlife left in S. Africa outside the Reserves but there I did see many buck droppings, and one evening coming back from the high pass into Lesotho I saw eight eland coming out of a drift in the distance in the setting sun. They are now very rare in that land of some poverty, being big and very good to eat. It was lovely to see them alive and in their natural setting.

On most of my visits the Grahams took me for several days touring in the car, and in this way we went to Knysna on the lagoon some four hundred miles west along the South coast, a historic area. From there we drove up on dirt roads into the Outeniqua and Gouna forests. Often we stopped the night at old farmhouses where the owners were glad to have people for dinner, bed and breakfast at very reasonable prices because their children were now grown-up and away. The food was always delicious, the beds comfortable, and one got such a warm welcome it was like staying with friends.

We stopped too at out of the way places for Donald to visit musical colleagues and deliver tapes and discs. One man who lived miles away in basic conditions up a cart track in the middle of nowhere, had an outstanding library of old, mostly Operatic recordings dating back to the days of acoustic and early electric recording; but he had no loo that worked. So we just took to the bush.

In 1989 I went out at the end of August ... Spring there, so that we could drive to Namaqualand four or five hundred miles away to see the marvellous wild flowers. These only appear for a few weeks after the rains and before the land reverts to semi desert. The West coast is much flatter at first with wide tracts of wheat on either side of the road. Then one comes to hills, mountain passes and rolling mists. But always one sees some cluster of lovely little flowers in a cleft. We stopped the first night at Clanwilliam, a pretty Cape-Dutch village with an excellent hotel, near a famous wildflower reserve. From there on mostly Afrikaans is spoken ... Boer-Dutch, not to be confused with African languages, of which there are many. The trouble is most people stick firmly to their own and speak nothing else, (which I sometimes feel may have caused much of the misunderstanding and mistrust over so many years) though all schoolchildren have to learn both if not three languages now.

We stopped for a picnic at one place where there was an historic cave up in the hill which Donald wanted to show me. Great men of bygone days had slept there when trekking and carved their names. The gate to the path was locked, and the only sign of life within miles was a tiny farmhouse with a metal windmill pumping water. It creaked eerily every time it went round. As we waited for Donald to return with the key I thought it must be one of the loneliest sounds and places in the world. The old wife who spoke only Afrikaans was alone there all day while her husband was out far away on the farm. One could not fail to admire the fortitude of these pioneer Boer descendants.

When we reached Namaqualand the flowers were spectacular. Sheets and sheets of orange, scarlet , blue, and white flowers of every shape and size: orange daisies, blue Felicias, scarlet arctotis, and mesembryanthemums of every hue, tall yellow bulbinellas and the tiny yellow cotulas like buttons which throw their equally tiny black shadows on the dust-coloured ground beneath. This is to mention but a few. We stayed at a small hotel, fairly basic, at Kamierskroon where the owner is an expert on the wild flowers and where best to find them each year. The country round about is lovely and very variable, but even at the copper mine at Nababeep a cataract of orange Namaqua daisies flowed down the grey shale and made wide rivulets of colour below. This was so striking I painted it but no-one here at home would know what it is. We drove for miles, taking picnics, and one saw few people about, black or white ...

basically it is sheep and goat country ... except once a little group of African school children out with their teacher walking through the daisies; a pretty sight.

There is nothing between the coast at that end of the great African continent and the Antarctic thousands of miles away. The Cape of Good Hope has always been known as the Cape of Storms, with strong currents and undertows. Many of the beaches are too dangerous for swimming, but the safe ones are marked and there are plenty of wide shallow bays.

Hermanus is a small fashionable seaside resort some eighty miles from Capetown, but even here the waves nearly tore my bathing suit off! We stayed with a charming elderly friend of the Grahams who had a big bungalow there; also an excellent African cook. He too was old, but the excellence varied, depending how drunk he had got on his 'days off'. When this happened – not often – Eileen would admonish him severely, but he always got his revenge by serving only three chops instead of four for dinner, or some such deed!

The original inhabitants of the Cape were the Bushmen and Hottentots, who were light brown in colour and quite different looking from the Bantu people further North. They unfortunately are now almost vanished races though one can still see traces of Hottentot blood in people today. Of the little Bushmen only a few remain in the desert regions of the North West.

Many Africans are wonderful subjects to paint with their widely varying features. There is much mixed blood among the Cape-Coloureds too, Malay and Indian. One who would have made a splendid picture was an African Nun in a white habit whom I saw at a Tchaikovsky concert in the City Hall. She was quite lovely.

Now South Africa is at the crossroads; white rule is almost at an end. It is a beautiful, for the most part clean, comparatively well run country apart from the racial discrepancies, but after so many years of sanctions and violence the economy is not good, and one considerable problem is the great number of illegal refugee Africans coming in from the much worse conditions in adjacent countries, causing much friction as local Africans fear losing their homes and jobs to refugees. Where will things go from here? Will moderate, enlightened African leaders be able to stem the flood, or will it go the same way as nearly every other Independent African country ... to ruin, corruption and tribal war. I love it so one can only hope and pray.

CHAPTER 20

THE MECHANICAL AGE

SAD TO SAY MY MECHANICAL KNOWLEDGE could only be described as nil. Having had a submariner father in the days of their infancy and therefore a brilliant mechanic, how can this be? I do not know, but many years of struggling with recalcitrant mowing and other machines since his death plus the gallant ministrations to them by friends and neighbours of the male sex have taught me much.

Now a whole new language for a whole new type of machine has been invented not one word of which appears in my grandfather's marvellous eight inches thick 140 years old dictionary, or even in my twenty-five year old one.

After those preliminary skirmishes with German and French tickets, my first confrontation with the new age machine was in Paris in the Jardin des Plantes, the great botanical gardens. It was pouring with rain and there was hardly a flower to be seen even in the extensive glass-houses. There were no people either; and absolutely no lavatory. My feet were soaking, and just as I was about to take to the bushes I met a young Frenchman and his girlfriend bent on the same goal. Then we noticed a discreet arrow saying Toilette.

Following a dripping path between bushes we came to a clearing with an amazing metal capsule in it; hermetically sealed. There was a small notice saying 'insert 10 francs', or some enormous sum, and 'do not remain inside for more than fifteen minutes'. What happened then it did not specify. Would we be encapsulated for life or simply find ourselves amongst the rats in the famous Paris sewers? We were pretty terrified, but also desperate. Eventually the girl agreed to go in if I stayed with the boyfriend outside. Then if she failed to reappear or the capsule went into orbit one of us could go for help and the other remain on the spot; (all this of course in French.)

Upon receiving the money an invisible door in the capsule slid open, sweet music played, in went the brave girl, and back slid the door. An agonised wait ensued. It was still raining. Would she be able to get out before the fifteen minutes were up or was fifteen minutes occupation compulsory we wondered?

Great was the relief when she finally appeared; but this was not the end of it. Before the door closed torrents of water flushed the loo, the wash basin, and might have given you a shower as well if you had not got out of the way. It also polished the seat. We watched in amazement until the music stopped and the whole thing sealed itself up again. Only then was it safe to insert another ten francs and go in myself, while the others gallantly waited. Any minute I felt it might take off my clothes and wash them too! At last, after all this was accomplished, we tottered to the nearest Bar and gulped several large cognacs.

Three years later I saw with horror on local television that a similar automatic 'toilet' had been installed in Belfast!, but sad to say, Sean, the newsreader announcing its arrival, did not give us a demonstration.

In 1980 I decided to install a burglar alarm. Living alone can sometimes be frightening; but I had already armed myself with a yacht siren...the sort ships use in fog. I bought it at a ship's chandler, and upon getting it home decided to see how it worked. I timidly pressed the button. The most stupendous bellow came forth ... goodness knows what the noise decibel was ... but a farmer friend peacefully ploughing his fields nearby almost fell off his tractor, and Robert Watson in his office not far away nearly had a heart attack. Every dog for miles around bolted or barked. We conferred, and decided it worked rather well.

Later I felt something more was needed for when I was away or out, so I had an extensive burglar alarm system installed as well. For years this frightened me more than any burglar. One only had quarter of a minute to get in and switch the thing off before all hell broke loose and policemen arrived in force. I had to run full tilt, and at night if the light was not on, invariable tripped over my dog's bone and other obstacles which increased the hazards.

The next year I went out to South Africa to stay with the Grahams who had also just installed a burglar alarm, because all their clothes had been stolen ... twice. Gladys, their Xhosa maid who came three times a week, was just as frightened of it as I was, and once I returned from a walk to find her sitting weeping on the doorstep, afraid to go in. I knew the feeling so well I gave her a big hug.

Worse was yet to come. After the success of 'Lydia's Story' the volume of letters, press notices and requests for another book grew more than I could manage by hand; my writing has always been illegible. On the advice of younger friends I bought a word processor, second-hand from a man in a neighbouring town. There were two huge books of instructions full of incomprehensible words telling one how to do unimaginable things.

Swahili, French, German and Italian … even a little Hindi I had quickly got somewhere with, but computer-speak proved really impossible.

The vendor tried most kindly to explain the basics, but he had quite a bad stammer. So, for twelve months this machine sat in a box on the floor and made me feel sick every time I looked at it, which was as seldom as possible.

By then my hands were becoming more and more painful with arthritis; it seemed the joints were worn out. I had merrily ridden horses that pulled like trains, helped my father cutting up trees with axe and saw, and heaved heavy luggage and furniture about all my life. Somehow one does not expect one's joints to wear out!

The Amstrad therefore was reluctantly promoted to a table and five weeks of torment began. All children from the age of six can work these things, but I did not have any children of six or otherwise. Finally I was rescued by two more neighbours, Frank and John, who took me and the machine in hand, reprogrammed both of us, and in no time at all it was writing letters and manuscript more or less as I meant it to!

'Play around with it' they said, 'Find out what it can do!'

'Ha, Ha, yes' I replied, having already had some nasty surprises, 'One day, in my second childhood perhaps!'

Basically I still feel like Lord L - - -, an eccentric young Peer, whom I occasionally met in the North of England as a girl when shooting with my father. It was told of him that when his super Bentley refused to start at the end of one day's shooting, he tried everything possible inside and then got out with the starting handle. His passenger thought he was going to crank it, but no, he proceeded to wallop the bonnet as hard as he could with the handle, after which he got in again no doubt feeling very much better! And waited for a tow.

I cannot wallop the Amstrad, it is well able to defend itself with a great collection of dirty tricks, like losing whole pages of toil, or letting one type away for hours and then putting up a smug green message saying 'Disc Full, cancel operation!'

Miraculously it has produced this book, and for the present my brain is full too. It cannot take in anything else. I have got to the end, and as the King said to Alice in Wonderland 'Begin at the beginning, go on to the end, and then Stop!' So as I have got to the end I must now stop … because I am leaving Coolattin, my beautiful home and garden, which I can no longer manage … forever. It was indeed another way of life.

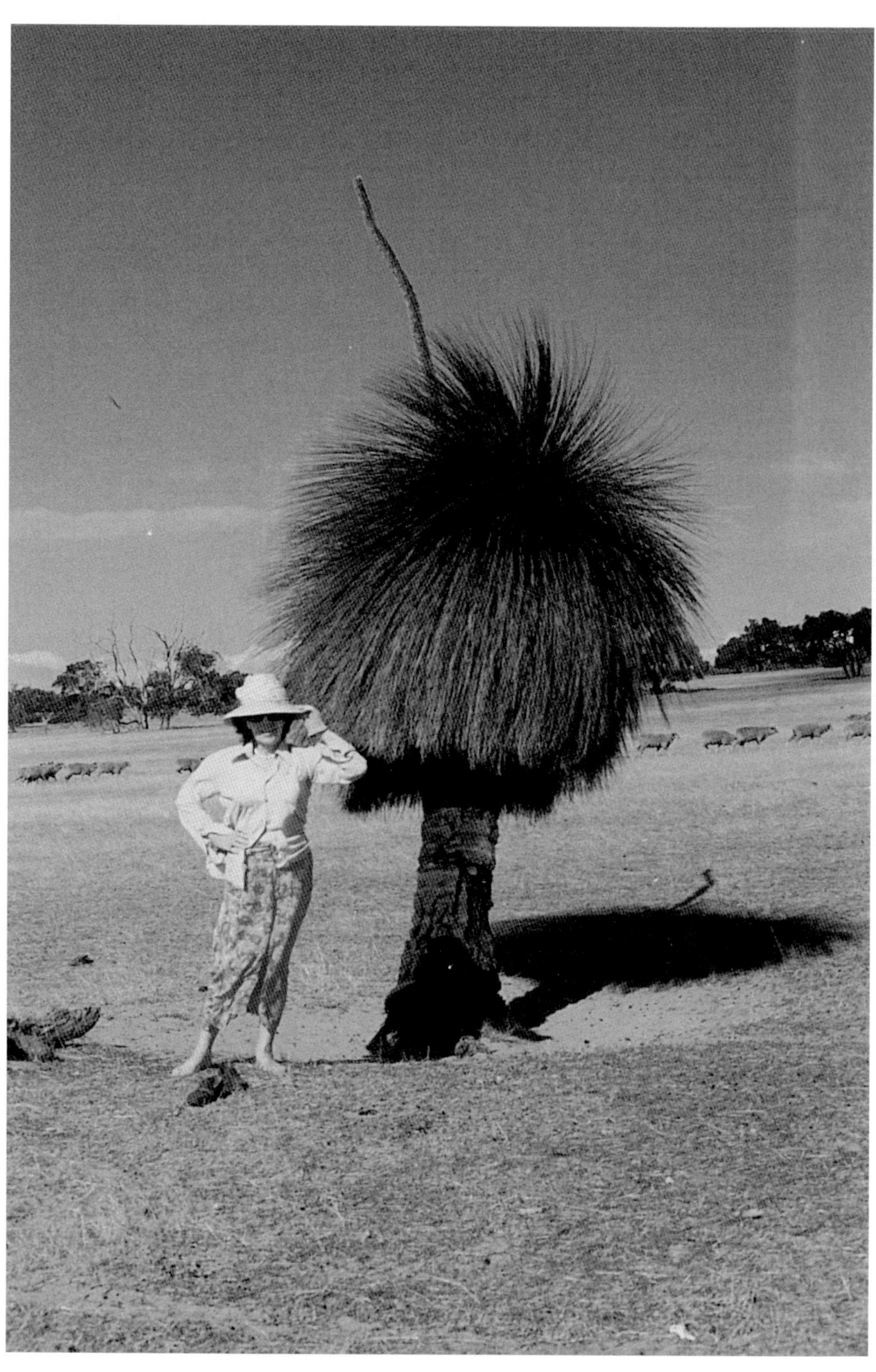

Lydia at the 'Blackboy' Grass Tree, Baramba

INDEX

Printed in Northern Ireland by Nicholson & Bass Ltd